BASEBALL IN THE BRONX, BEFORE THE YANKEES

Gregory Christiano

PublishAmerica
Baltimore

Softcover 9781630048945
PUBLISHED BY PUBLISHAMERICA, LLLP
www.publishamerica.com
Baltimore

Printed in the United States of America

Dedicated to the memory of my father Ulderico, a native of the Bronx, whose love of baseball stirred my passion and devotion to the game.

Contents

ILLUSTRATIONS AND PHOTOGRAPHS

PROLOGUE

Every baseball fan knows of the greatest franchise in the game – The New York Yankees. They are also known as The Bronx Bombers; appropriately named because they happen to reside in the Bronx, the northernmost borough of New York City. After the founding of the American League in 1901, the Baltimore Orioles, one of the original clubs to join the league, moved to New York two years later. The new owners secured a piece of land on Broadway between 165th and 168th Streets and quickly built a field that was named Hilltop Park. Being one of the highest points in Manhattan, the nickname Highlanders was chosen for the new team. However, sportswriters referred to them as the Yankees, or Yanks. It was much easier to type and fit in the headlines. In 1923, the team moved to their newly built park in the Bronx. The rest is history.

In the years preceding the Yankees, the Bronx was part of Westchester County. In 1873 the western section of the Bronx (the area west of the Bronx River and south of the City of Yonkers) which consisted of the Towns and Villages of Mott Haven, Morrisania, Kingsbridge and West Farms was annexed by the City and County of New York.[1] This area was initially called the 'Northern Annex,' or the 'Annexed District.'

By 1895 the eastern Bronx (mostly the Town of Westchester and portions of the Town of Eastchester and Pelham) were also annexed from Westchester County. A year later, City Island, in the Town of Pelham also joined the District. This was the make-up of the Bronx in the latter part of the nineteenth century. By 1898, the City of New York was consolidated into the Five Boroughs.

Baseball was played throughout New York in its earliest forms. People were born into a fan base and there was no switching sides. It became everyone's birthright. We all had a team to root for. People were identified with that team, like a nationality, religion or class.

One of the themes of early baseball's development was the central role of New York City and vicinity in nurturing and spreading the infant game. Virtually all the best baseball was played in and around New York. The Bronx and its teams contributed to that development.

From the 1830s through the late 1850s America played an assortment of ball and bat games. Each city and region boasted its own variation. When the Knickerbocker rules standardized the game, many of those teams adopted those rules. By 1856 *Porter's Spirit of the Times* reported that baseball players had converted every grassy lot within a ten mile radius of New York City into playing fields. Brooklyn was asserted as being the "city of baseball clubs." And this Cambrian-like explosion of clubs was because of the sheer popularity the game had achieved with the citizens of the region. They journeyed in droves to attend any matches advertised:

> "Yesterday the cars of the Second and Third avenue Railroads were crowded for hours with the lovers of ball playing, going out to witness the long-talked of match between the "Gotham" and "Knickerbocker" Clubs. We think the interest to see this game was greater than any other match ever played." - **"Base Ball Match,"** *New York Daily Times*, September 6, 1856, page 8.

The *Times* account includes a box score detailing "hands out" and "runs" for each player. The text uses "aces" as well as "runs," and employs the term "inning," not "innings." It notes players who "made some splendid and difficult catches in the long field."

Improvements in transportation and communication in the antebellum era had begun to create a more unified and national culture and fueled the spread of the game. That half-decade before the 1860 presidential election saw the clear enthusiastic embrace of the modern version of baseball in the Mid-Atlantic States and to a great extent the entire nation. On December 5, 1856, the *New York Mercury* coined the phrase, "the national pastime." The term was picked up as the game spread across the land. But its roots lay in New York City and surrounding towns and municipalities. Morrisania (a section of the Bronx) was part of this fledgling pastime.

Baseball developed into more than just a boy's game. It became a repository of national ideals of fair play, sportsmanship, rule of law (being objectively enforced by an impartial judge - the umpire), equal opportunity (each side gets a turn at bat), demonstration of teamwork where the individual could excel. What better symbol can it represent that is all good in American way of life? From a mild exercise, it set standards for each player to develop good judgment, skill and endurance in their quest for gamesmanship and fair competition. The general folk took civic pride, adopted role models among the players which lead to hero worship. Baseball gave many a connecting sentiment, a feeling of belonging. Intense and often remarkably similar emotions are to this day evoked by the game. Baseball is cyclical like the seasons, generational, passing from father to son, and repetitive, it has a long and almost sacred history we can follow and recognize from one generation to the next. It became a birthright. But, as in life, there was ultimately corruption; drinking, gambling and game fixing was rife. But it didn't destroy the spirit of the game. Baseball survived and prospered.

"This is the last pure place where Americans dream. This is the last great arena, the last green arena, where everybody can learn lessons of life." - Marcus Giamatti in the Houston Post (April 9, 1990, Bart's Son Partially Quoting his Father).

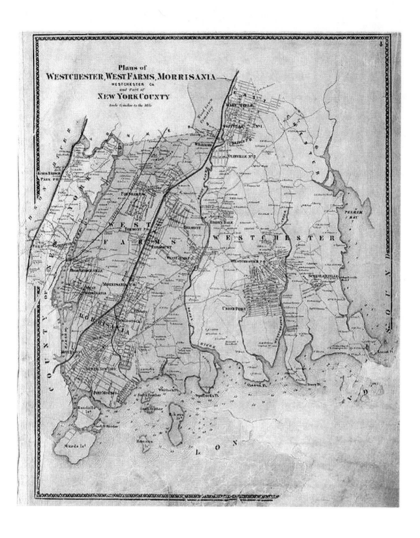

The Bronx - 1867

THE MORRISANIA UNIONS

Before the Yankees arrived in the Bronx, baseball had been played there for decades. One of the more well-known and prominent amateur teams was the **Union Base Ball Club of Morrisania.** Popularly known as the **Morrisania Unions.** [This was a time when baseball was spelled as two words, and fans were called 'cranks']. They were organized, Tuesday evening, July 17, 1855 with 23 active members. The members of these early clubs were mostly young gentlemen who were professional tradesmen, merchants and businessmen, out for some athletic enterprise. [A baseball club of the 1850s was in every sense a club – formed by groups of men attracted together in social or working conditions who also shared an interest in the game]. They met for practice, or what they called 'field exercise, 'every Monday and Friday afternoons at 5 o'clock. They played only one game their first year and defeated the Young Americans of Harlem, New York, by a score of 25 to 8.

Thomas E. Sutton (b. 1812) was their first president. He operated a printing house in lower Manhattan and was a member of Fire Engine #25, during the great fire of 1835. [2] He was one of the six original organizers: Senator William Cauldwell* (Secretary); Ed Albrow, of the Knickerbocker Fire Insurance Company; Ed White who had a large estate in the town; John L. Burnett, real estate and insurance agent, and Henry J. Ford, 'a retired gentleman of English birth.'[3] Today, Morrisania is a neighborhood in the southwestern section of the Bronx. In the mid nineteenth century it was a separate municipality in Westchester County. It ran north to 8th Street, (now 165th Street) and south to Harlem Bridge.

The Morrisania Unions of 1867 – 1868
*The players are (left-to-right): George Smith, LF; Dan
Ketchum, 3B; Tommy Beals, RF; Ed Shelly, 3B; Dave
Birdsall, C; Charley Pabor, P; Albro Aiken, SS; Henry
Austin, CF; Al Martin, 2B and John Goldie, 1B*

*William Cauldwell, born 1824 played ball in
lower Manhattan, went to primary school at the High
School for Males at No. 36 Crosby near Broome
Street. After moving to Louisiana he returned in 1848
and settled in Morrisania. As editor of the weekly
Sunday Mercury, New York, Cauldwell made mention
of baseball on May 1, 1853 and later that year devoted
space to the Knickerbockers – Gotham match of
July. He was the first baseball reporter (active prior
to Henry Chadwick). He served as New York State
Senator (Democrat) – the 9th District (1868 – 1871).

Was delegate to the Democratic National Convention from New York, 1888. He became the first secretary of the Union Club.

WM. CAULDWELL.

William Cauldwell – 1860
(One of the founders of the Morrisania Unions)

Thomas E. Sutton was the president of the club for the first three years, and then D.E. Milliken held the office afterward for the next seven years. By 1866 the presiding officer was G. H. Albro [Ed Albrow?] under whose regime the club attained an eminence it had never reached before.

The Unions played their games at the Triangle, on a lot behind what was known as Fisher's coal yard (now 163rd Street.) It was named Melrose Station Grounds less than a mile from present day Yankee Stadium. In 1868 they moved to Tremont and Arthur Avenues, and there they built their first enclosed baseball grounds. The price of admission was 25 cents. Ed Wright was the cashier, and Thomas Sutton's son, T. Emery Sutton, had the distinction of collecting the very first quarter. There was no grand stand, only board seats. The professional baseball leagues had not yet been organized.

Extremely rare, early, and remarkably significant trophy ball from an 1859 match between two of the greatest teams of the era, the Union of Morrisania (based in the Bronx) and the Excelsiors of Brooklyn. Both of these clubs were charter members of the National Association of Base Ball Players (NABBP). This gold-painted "lemon-peel" ball commemorates a victory by the Unions and is lettered "1859 / Oct 5 / Union 19 / Excelsior 15 / 9 Innings"

The Morrisania Unions played when baseball was in its infancy. The usual prize awarded the winning club in a championship match was a ball with which the game was played. The ball was coated with silver (or gold-painted) over which was inscribed the teams' names, score and date, and kept as a trophy. In those early years, these trophies were displayed in a large case in Morrisania Hall (at old 5th Street and Fourth Avenue) by a fellow named Louis Combs. [By 1898 the Morrisania Hall was located at 117th Street and 3rd Ave.] [4] The team made occasional trips through the country. Funds to help pay for their expenses were donated by the townspeople. The players were gone for two to three weeks at a time.

What was the nature of the game being played in those days? Alexander Cartwright is widely credited with publishing the first set of baseball rules for his 1845 New York Knickerbockers which evolved into baseball as we know it today. Other teams published their own rules as well. These rules differed and this led to confusion and disagreements. For instance, the removal of the "soaking" rule (throwing the ball at the runner to get the out) allowed the Knickerbockers to develop a harder baseball that was more like a cricket ball. Remember, these guys were playing with no gloves; no equipment to protect the catcher. Catching a pitched ball on a bounce, the catcher stood 10 to 12 feet behind home plate keeping a safe distance from getting clobbered by a foul ball. There was only one umpire, with very little to do. The first umpires sat at a table along the third base line. Their main duties consisted of keeping the scorebook, calling balls fair or foul, and settling any disputes that might arise between the teams. They would not take a more active role until the late 1850s.

The pitching box (no mound as yet) was only 45 feet from home. Today's pitching standard of 60'-6" was not established until 1893, when the first pitching rubber was introduced. There was no defined batter's box. The striker, or batter, was allowed to run toward or backpedal from the ball after it left the pitcher's hand. The official batter's box was not introduced until 1860, the same year that running toward or away from the pitch was banned. In 1857, the distance between bases was officially set at 90'. The bases were similar in appearance to what is in use today, but home plate was actually a 9" to 12" circular metal plate. There were many other rules and dynamics of the game that have been changed over the course of baseball's history, (see notes).

In 1856, Daniel 'Doc' Adams, President of the Knickerbockers submitted a resolution asking that interested teams should meet at a convention to draw up common rules. The convention was held on January 22, 1857 and was attended by sixteen teams from New York State (mostly from Manhattan, and Long Island.)*

*Two years before this historic meeting there was an attempt to formulate standard rules according to an account in the *New York Daily Tribune*, Monday, December 10, 1855, pg. 7, col. 2:

"Base-Ball Club Convention. – A Convention of representatives from a number of Base-Ball Clubs met at "The Gotham" public house in the Bowery on Friday evening. There are fourteen or fifteen of those organizations in New-York and Brooklyn, beside three in Jersey City and four in Newark; of which eight were represented on Friday evening by committees and several others by letters. T.C. Van Cott of "The

Gotham" presided, and Mr. Cornell of the Baltic Club was Secretary. The object of the Convention is to make arrangements for a banquet and ball, and to establish general rules for the various clubs. Without taking definite action on those matters the Convention adjourned, to meet at the same place on Saturday evening, the 15 inst., to give opportunity for a more general representation of the various Clubs."

Adams changed the length of the game to nine equal innings, instead of declaring the first team to score 21 "aces" or runs, the winner. Adams also ruled that five innings must be played to be declared a game.

It was agreed that they would meet each March and it was at the next meeting in 1858, the National Association of Base Ball Players (NABBP) was created. [By 1860, the meeting date was changed to December].The Unions of Morrisania was one of the original charter members.(The Unions also were to join the New-York State Association of Base-Ball Players in November 1867. See details in Appendix I.) The rules that were adopted by the NABBP became known as 'The New York Game.' This eventually evolved into modern day baseball. The Unions played the local teams from their inception right through the Civil War. [The games were not played by any formal schedule, rather by written invitation from one club secretary to the other. The inviting team acted as hosts and supplied the entertainment.] Many teams were reduced in number or disbanded because members joined the army. The war depleted the rosters everywhere and the numbers of teams in the NABBP dwindled from 59 in 1860 to 34 by 1865. The Unions were no exception and were affected. The number of games they played were very few each season:

Here's their won-lost record through the War:

1861 3 – 1 (5th place)
1862 5 – 5 (4th place)
1863 3 – 3 -
1864 4 – 3 -
1865 13 – 10 (3rd place) [The teams reorganized and their rosters back to full strength. By December 1866 the ranks swelled to 91 clubs. The play dates were picking up].

The lineup for an 1862 game with the Excelsiors:

UNION
Durell, 1b
Abrams, c
Hannegan, p
Hyatt, 3b
Bassford, lf
Nicholson, rf
Pinckney, 2b
Collins, cf
Gaynor, ss

A footnote here: the batteries for the Excelsiors were Jim Creighton pitching, Joe Leggett, catching…two superstars of this era. The Unions won that game in 6 innings, 12 – 4, called because of a rain storm. [5]

Baseball was poised for a great boom that followed the War. The period 1865 to 1870 is most pivotal and a number of factors and people contributed to its growth and popularity from a relatively localized activity to a nationwide phenomenon.

New York Tribune, August 21, 1865, pg 8 [four months after Lee's surrender at Appomattox Court House, Virginia, essentially ending the American Civil War]:

UNION
Hudson, rf
Smith, 1b
Durell, lf
Hannegan, ss
Nicholson, 3b
Birdsall, c
Ketchum, cf
Pabor, p
"Sam", p

The *New York Times* of Wed. Aug. 28, 1867 (the Unions' championship year), records the lineup of the club:

John Goldie, lf
Al Martin, 2b
Charlie Pabor, p
Henry Austin, cf
Akbro Aiken, ss
Birdsall, c
Ketchum, 3b
Tommy Beals, rf
Smith, 1b

Their won-lost record for that year (1867) was 21 − 8. [6] On July 31st, the Unions soundly defeated the defending champion, Brooklyn Atlantics, 32 − 19. In their rematch, October 10th, it was curtains for the Atlantics. After Brooklyn took an 11 – 9 lead at the top of the seventh, the Unions scored three in the bottom of the inning. The Brooklyn team tied it in the top of the eight, but the Unions took the advantage back with two runs of their own. Trailing by two entering the ninth, the Atlantics could score only one and lost 14 – 13. Charlie Pabor was the winning pitcher. And so the NABBP championship which the Atlantics held so long was wrested from their grasp! It was a glorious victory for the Unions.

The uniforms of the period were pretty nifty. The 1867 champion Unions wore a distinctive style: A blue cap and pants; trimmings in red; white shirt, trimmed with blue; a stylized letter 'U' on this bib-designed shirt and a tri-colored web belt.

***Fire Brigade Belt adopted by the
Morrisania Union Club 1850s***

[During the 1850s, belts were the single defining characteristic of a team's uniform and most were similar in style and color. These belts were the only garment players wore bearing the club's name. As such, they were often quite elegant and striking in design, and a symbol of team pride. While they are very prominently featured in various equipment catalogs for sale, very few nineteenth-century baseball belts, especially those dating to the 1850s, have actually survived. The early connection between fire companies and baseball is the reason many early baseball uniforms were designed in the style of fire uniforms (often displaying a shield design on the front of the jersey). As a cost-cutting move, members would then use the belts from their fire uniforms with their baseball uniforms. For that reason, many early nineteenth-century firefighters' belts are indistinguishable from baseball belts.]

They had turned semi-pro in 1866 and fully professional by 1870. (The dedication to amateurism was long since challenged as early as 1860 when superstar players like Jim Creighton* were being paid for their services. By 1862, with the opening of the first enclosed ballpark in Brooklyn, professionalism really took off. Now these fenced-in parks enabled the owners of the grounds to charge admission. This gave incentive for the teams to buy professional players, become a noteworthy enterprise and draw the paying crowds.) The Unions also benefited by this when they opened their own enclosed park in 1868 and charged admission. [7] An early report in the *Brooklyn Daily Eagle*, July 28, 1862, extols the virtues of amateurism:

"Base ball is a recreation, not a business, and should be played for the amusement and health it affords, and not for the triumphs that may be gained over this or that set of players. There is far too much of this great desire to win matches prevalent for the best interest of the game, and when we see a game played in the spirit it should be, we like to make the fact prominent so that others may profit thereby."

Won-Lost record from the Unions' post-war seasons:

1866   25 – 3 (1st place)
1867   21 – 8 (3rd place, but won the playoffs and beat the Brooklyn Atlantics for the championship)
1868   37 – 6 (3rd place)
1869   5 - 10 (5th place, the Pro team, Cincinnati Red Stockings were in the NABBP)
1870   7 – 18 against professional teams
1870   20 – 19 through the rest of the season

The next year, the Unions refused to enter NABBP which was created by new fifteen pro teams. That year, the NABBP folded and the new National Association of Professional Base Ball Players (NAPBBP) was founded (1871 – 1875). The Unions disbanded in 1873. But they left behind a solid legacy which played an important role in the origins, spread and popularity of our national pastime.

THE BALL PLAYERS

Who were these men, these early pioneers of the game? Some went on to become stellar baseball players for the professional clubs in the National Association and later the National League. Many faded into obscurity, just a name in a record book. But their careers began with the Morrisania Unions. Here are a few of them:

Henry Austin

Henry Austin (1844 – 1895). Not too much is known about him other than he played on the team as center fielder from 1865 to 1870.

John Elias Bass (1848, Charleston, South Carolina – September 25, 1888, Denver, Colorado) Bass played shortstop for the Unions for only one year in 1870 and left the team turning professional at shortstop in the major leagues from 1871-1877. He played for the Cleveland Forest Citys (sic), Brooklyn Atlantics, and the Hartford Dark Blues.

In 1871, he led the National Association of Professional B.B.Players in triples with ten.

Estaban Bellan

Esteban 'Steve' Bellan (October 1, 1849 – August 8, 1932). The Havana-born Bellán studied at St. John's College in the Bronx from 1866 to 1868, now known as Fordham University. He joined the school's baseball team, already having learned the game before coming to New York, when American sailors brought the game to Cuba. After graduating in 1868, at age 18, Bellán played one season for the Union of Morrisania and was part of their national championship team in 1868. He joined the Troy Haymakers in 1869 and continued playing for the team when they joined the NAPBBP when it was formed in 1871 to replace the NABBP ceased operations.

After leaving the Mutuals in 1873, he moved back to Cuba to play in their newly formed baseball leagues. His team, Club Habana, defeated Club Matanzas, 51 to 9 on December 27, 1874, in the first organized baseball game ever played in Cuba. He later became the club's player-manager, from 1878 to 1886, and led them to three Cuban League championships. He has been called the true "father" of Cuban baseball, for his role organizing the first Cuban baseball game, his success as a player and manager, as well as his continued influence on the game after his career had ended.

Tommy Beals

Thomas Lamb Beals (August 1850 – October 2, 1915) Played one season for the Unions in their championship year of 1867. He moved on to play mostly in the outfield and at second base for the Washington Olympics, Washington Blue Legs, and Chicago White Stockings from 1871 to 1880. With Chicago he hit a career-low .152, and hung up his spikes after the season.

Charles S. Bierman (1845 – August 4, 1879) Played first base for one year, 1870. He then went on to play one game for the Fort Wayne Kekiongas, the following year going hitless in two at bats, had one walk, and committed two errors at first base. Bierman died in his hometown of Hoboken, New Jersey. [There was a Bearman, spelled this way, who joined the Union Club in 1868]. [8]

David Birdsall

David Solomon Birdsall (July 16, 1838 – December 30, 1896) Caught for the Unions from 1863 to 1868 left the team and then rejoined the Unions in 1870. He went on to play in the National Association of Professional Base Ball Players from 1871 to 1873.

First Baseball Card? A photo of Dave Birdsall which was up for auction (2008) was identified as possibly the first baseball card classified in that category (authenticated by the Wentz Brothers of BMW Sportscards who did the research and identified the card). Birdsall was playing for the Unions when this photo was taken nicknaming him "The Old Man." [A nickname and term of respect he earned for being the oldest veteran on the team.] This was also verified at the Robert Edward Auctions for 2008. They are researchers and cataloguers of rare and historically significant items

Dave Birdsall was with the Unions of Morrisania before joining Harry Wright's famous Cincinnati Red Stockings in 1869 Reference to Birdsall's nickname "The Old Man" is cited in When *Johnny Comes Sliding Home: The Post-Civil War Baseball Boom, 1865-1870* by William Ryczek. It is also referred to in *The Minor League Milwaukee Brewers, 1859-1952* by Brian Podoll, which explains that the Unions star pitcher Charley Pabor's eccentric but sunny disposition earned him the curious nickname "The Old Woman in the Red Cap," one of baseball's most notable nicknames from any era. It is also explained that his battery-mate, catcher Dave Birdsall, was his diametric opposite in disposition and was known as "The Old Man." These nicknames poked fun at the fact that as pitcher and catcher, this unlikely pair was as inseparable as a married couple, despite being totally at odds with one another in terms of personality. A similar card of Charley Pabor may surface some day with his nickname on it. It is possible that such a card was produced but none have survived.

Circa 1866-1870 carte-de-visite
"The Old Man" - The First Baseball Card?

Using artworks (even detailed woodcuts) for identification purposes Robert Edwards staff consulted with several baseball scholars. [I don't know exactly how this card was issued, but it was clearly mass-produced, and I'm pretty sure it was in 1865. Everything about the style points to this card being from 1865, and most likely reproduced from a woodcut engraving. The woodcut was published in November 1865, so the photograph that was used to create it had to exist before that date. Both the woodcut and the CDV (**carte-de-visite***) image are clearly created from the very same photographic image and pose. The woodcut is pure artwork while the CDV photograph is an artist-enhanced photographic image (enhanced in the photo as made, not on the surface of the CDV) which used the same original photograph (probably a salt print) to create it.] There was a consensus and they could find no dissenting opinion that this was Dave Birdsall. This research was verified by Brian and Mike Wentz and thus allowed them to present this extremely important card. Is this The First Baseball Card? Not everyone agrees on the definition of a card, so whenever scholars look at the earliest cards, they try to qualify the definition. The answer to that question really depends on how one defines a card. It does have some very important and unique qualities that in the opinion of most baseball historians make the card seriously worthy of consideration for the title. It is the only card from this early era that was ever seen featuring the image of a specific current player who is identified on the card. These are generally recognized as defining characteristics for baseball cards, dating from the 1880s all the way up to modern cards. The famous 1863 Jordan Marsh CDV photograph of Harry Wright is an extraordinary card, but does not identify Harry Wright as part of the design of the card. The famous Jim Creighton memorial Peck & Snyder trade card is not dated, but the biography on the reverse makes very clear it was issued after his passing.

So there is a significant distinction to Birdsall's "The Old Man" card. He was alive. He was a current active player. He is identified on the card. To the best of their knowledge, Birdsall's card is the very first baseball card with the identification of a current individual player incorporated into the design of the card. By this definition, the "The Old Man" card can lay claim to being the first baseball card. Not everyone will agree that this is the first baseball card, that even attempting to declare what is the first baseball card can be controversial, but the next time there is discussion or a debate about the issue, "The Old Man" is at least worthy of consideration for the title. Whether this card dates from 1866, believed based on the "Unions" bib style, or as late as 1870 (the year of Birdsall's last season with the Unions after spending the 1869 season with the Red Stockings), the next oldest baseball card(s) with a traditional design, featuring the identified image of an individual player, were issued by Old Judge tobacco in 1886. This card was sold for $8,812.50.

* **Carte-de-visite** was a type of small photograph which was patented in Paris, France by photographer Andre Adolphe Disderi 1854, although first used by Louis Dodero.It was usually made of an albumen print which was a thin paper photograph mounted on a thicker paper card.

Alfred "Count" Gedney

Alfred "Count" Gedney (May 10, 1843 – March 26, 1922) In 1870 he was the regular left fielder for Morrisania. He spaned four seasons (1872 – 1875) with the NAPBBP – Troy Haymakers (1872), N.Y. Mutuals (1875), Brooklyn Eckfords (1872) and the Philadelphia Athletics (1874).

Bernard J. Hanigan (also spelled Hannegan) (aka: Berney Hanigan) (birth and death unknown) He entered the club around 1859, and the following year became the pitcher until service in the army. He was a great favorite with his teammates and what's more, the most popular player in the club with the ladies of the village who would flock in great numbers to the Union grounds when the games were in progress.

Creighton's legend shined great for many years, and for serious baseball historians his legend will shine greatly forever. More than three years after his death, on November 4, 1865, the highly respected *Frank Leslie's Illustrated Newspaper* issued a two-page foldout woodcut intended for home display that was a tribute to his memory. Surrounding Creighton's larger portrait were identified woodcut images of seventeen of the leading players of the day. Hanigan was pictured second from the left at the bottom. According to many sources, he was always very proud to have been chosen to be among these elite baseball players representing the highest level of organized play at this early time in the history of the game.

Berney's characteristics as a ballplayer was his "coolness under ill circumstances." According to a portrait of him the *The Daily Graphic,* New York, Nov. 6, 1866 [an illustrated evening newspaper], he was said to have a "quiet, gentlemanly demeanor. As short-stop he has few equals and is a first-class batsman…" His particular style was described as being short, sharply-hit grounders. In the field he was noted to make exceptional fly catches, had good judgment at taking 'high balls' and was called "the most gentlemanly ball player in the fraternity." He apparently excelled at what he did both in batting and fielding. He was a star in every respect. He left the club in 1866.

Richard 'Dick' Higham (1851 – 1905) one of the most colorful characters who ever played for the Unions. Born in

Ipswich, Suffolk, England, his family immigrated to the U.S. when he was two and settled in Hoboken, New Jersey. He was a very versatile player, playing second base for the Unions in 1870. He joined the new professional National Association a year later. He had no love of the game as time would reveal.

In an era when the average span of a professional player's career was perhaps six seasons, Dick Higham played for eleven years. By the time of the founding of the National League, his playing career was more than half over. At the conclusion of his time with the Troy Trojans in 1880, he remained in Troy, New York. In 1881, he became a National League umpire. He was accused of fixing games and gambling. Higham outlined a simple code—if the gambler received a telegram from him saying "Buy all the lumber you can," the gambler was to bet on Detroit. No telegram meant that the gambler was to bet on his opponent. A private detective hired by the Detroit Wolverines owner proved his collusion and as a result of this evidence, Higham was fired as an umpire and banned from baseball. To date, he is the only umpire to have been banished from the game.

James "Jim" Holdsworth (July 14, 1850 – March 22, 1918) Nicknamed "Long Jim," he played shortstop for seven different professional teams in his nine year career. Was a member of the Morrisania club for only one year – 1870. He's buried in Woodlawn Cemetery, Bronx.

John J. Kenney (1844 – August 7, 1893) Played outfield and second base for the Brooklyn Atlantics (1867 – 1869, 1872) Played the outfield and infield for Morrisania for one year, 1870.

Albert DeGroot Martin (Sept. 1847– April 1, 1926) He played second base for the Unions from 1866 to 1868, 28 games in each of those years. After taking a couple of years off, he played second base and the outfield for the 1872 Brooklyn Eckfords and the 1874-1875 Brooklyn Atlantics. He was also known as Albert May.

Charles Pabor

Charles Henry "Charlie" Pabor (September 24, 1846 – April 23, 1913), also spelled Charley, had a unique nickname – "The Old Woman in the Red Cap." Pabor pitched for the Unions from 1865 through the championship seasons of '67 and '68. Dropping out for a year, he rejoined the team in 1870. Born in Brooklyn, he played his early baseball in and around the New York City area. After his stint with the

Unions, he joined the Cleveland Forest Citys (sic) of the National Association as a left fielder and manager. On May 4, 1871, Charles managed and played while batting 0 for 4 in the first game of the season, which is considered the first professional game ever played, between his Forest Citys and the Fort Wayne Kekiongas.

After the 1875 season ended, and the demise of the National Association, he quit baseball altogether and stayed in New Haven, Connecticut, joining their police department, where he enjoyed a long career. Charlie died in New Haven of pneumonia at the age of 66.

A carte-de-visite of legendary baseball-maker John Van Horn.

John Van Horn (no dates), John Van Horn was a former ballplayer and professional shoemaker in New York, who became the leading producer of baseballs during the 1850s and 1860s. He supplied the Knickerbocker Club among others and has been dubbed the "greatest ball maker of the 19th century."

Prior to the mass production of baseballs, each one was hand-made and consisted of rubber twisted into a round shape with any solid substance, such as a rock, at its core. It was covered with yarn and then with leather or cloth. Needless to say, the quality and consistency of these early balls varied considerably. In the mid-1850s, two men, Harvey Ross, a sail maker who was a member of the Atlantics, and John Van Horn, a member of the Union of Morrisania, began manufacturing baseballs on a regular basis. Van Horn took rubber strips from the old shoes in his shop and cut them up tp provide the center for his baseballs.

Not much is known about Van Horn personally, other than he was a shoemaker by trade and a second baseman for the Union Club of Morrisania in the 1850s (there is also a reference to him playing for the Baltic Club of New York).

George Wright

George Wright (January 28, 1847 – August 21, 1937). By far the most renowned person who ever played for Morrisania has to be George Wright. He was a pioneer in the sport. Early in the summer of 1866, Wright moved from catcher for Gotham, which played eight NABBP matches that year, to shortstop for the Unions playing in 28 games. He left the team after the season, and then returned two years later.

1868 was a banner year for George Wright where he demonstrated his superlative talent. The highlights of that season for George and the team are remarkable.

In that year, Wright won the Clipper Medal for being the best shortstop in baseball. [On April 25th, the *New York Clipper,* a sports newspaper, announced that it would give a

Gold Ball of regulation weight and size to the club proclaimed champions of 1868. In addition, medals will be awarded to the nine best players at their positions.]

May 12th 1868, the second all-star game of the year was held between players selected from the New York and Brooklyn clubs. New York had only 8 players and went without a shortstop, but George was asked to play for New York. They lasted till the 11th inning before losing 36-33 to Brooklyn. June 1st of that year, the Champion Unions, with George at shortstop, played their first game of the season winning, 31-16, over the Olympic Club of Paterson, NJ.

On June 6, the Champion Unions were almost upset by a team of Yale students in New Haven, and needed 2 runs in the last of the 9th to tie, and 2 in the last of the 10th to win, 16-14.

On August 6, 1868, the Unions, on their Western tour, travelled to Chicago where a large crowd saw the Champions defeat the Atlantic Club of Chicago 41-12. George Wright and John Goldie each scored 7 runs.

Aug. 25, 1868 - In Cincinnati, the Union club lost their first game after 25 straight victories, including a 12-8 win over the local Red Stockings. The next day, the Cincinnati Reds club wins, 13-12. Harry Wright, his elder brother, played shortstop for the Reds while George plays for the Unions.

On Oct 6, in a match that decided the Championship of 1868, the Atlantics pound the Unions, 24-8, at Morrisania.

In 1869 he left the Unions to join his brother Harry on the Red Stockings, earning $1,400 (some sources recorded $1,800) his first year with the club. Possessing dashing good looks, George was particularly popular with female fans, who were known to scandalously lift their skirts to reveal their red-stockinged ankles in George's presence.

On April 22, 1876, Wright became the first batter in National League history, and grounded out to the shortstop. Brother Harry managed the Red Stockings and made George his right hand man. The brothers are now both in the Baseball Hall of Fame. George was inducted in 1937, Harry in 1953.

RANK AND FILE MORRISANIA BALL PLAYERS
(Years played and positions)

William Abrams.................1859, 1860, 1862 - 1867, 3b, of
Albro Aken.....................1866 - 1867, lf, c, ss
Henry Austin................... 1865 - 1870, cf
John Bass......................... 1870, ss
Tommy Beals................... 1867, rf
Steve Bellan.....................1868, 2b, rf
Charlie Bierman................1870, 1b
Dave Birdsall...................1863 - 1868, 1870, c
Brown............................. 1870, 1b
Al Gedney....................... 1870, lf
John Goldie..................... 1866 - 1869, 1b
Bernard Hannegan............1859, 1860, 1862 - 1866, ss, of
Dick Higam..................... 1870, 2b
Jim Holdsworth................1870, 3b

W. F. Hudson...................1864 - 1867, rf, 3b, of
John Kenney...................1870, 3b, of
Dan Ketchum...................1865 - 1867, of, 2b, 3b
Al Martin.........................1866 - 1868, 2b, of
Norton..............................1867, p
Charlie Pabor...................1865 - 1868, 1870, p
Reynolds.........................1868 - 1870, of
Ed Shelley.......................1868, 1870, 3b, 2b
George Smith...................1865 - 1869, infield, of
George Wright..................1866, 1868, ss, c, 2b

There were other less well known members of the Union club – John Goldie, playing 1b, 1866-'69; Reynolds - rf, 1868 – '70; Ed Shelly - 3b and 2b, 1868 and '70; George Smith - lf, 1b, 1865 – '69; John Bass – ss, 1870; Some 1863 players: Nicholson, lf; Abrams, ss; Pinckney, 2b; Albio, rf; O'Donnell, 1b; O'Byrne, cf. There were many others. [See appendix III for rosters and lineups for the Unions].They all had their story. They spent their youth playing a game they loved, for no high paying salaries, no brass bands heralding their exploits, no commercial endorsements, on primitive playing fields and with little or no equipment. They played on their own leisure time for the sheer pleasure and excitement of it. Their lives and deeds on the field have been immortalized in the legacy they left us.

Other Clubs in the Bronx

There's not much information concerning another Morrisania team known as The Enterprise Junior Base Ball Club, other than they played three games in 1856.[9] A junior club consisted of lads from 15 to 18 years old. Any player over 18 played the senior circuit. The club turned senior in 1858 with only one game recorded on October 23rd of that year. After that, they seemed to have disappeared. No mention of them has been found thus far.

There were many other amateur clubs playing in the Bronx during those formative years, but little information is attainable on them: The Jerome Park Base Ball Club (Sept., 1867), their grounds were the Jerome Park Race Course (west of Bedford Park, north of Fordham).They are mentioned in the schedule from Sports and Pastimes Base-Ball section in the *Brooklyn Daily Eagle* of August 10, 1867:

**"Aug 10 – Oriental vs. Jerome Park,
on Red House grounds, Harlem."**

The Buena Base Ball Club of Mott Haven was another short-lived franchise. Their one recorded game was played August 30, 1860 in which they defeated the Newark Jrs., 39 – 21. [10] No mention of them after 1861, probably disbanded because of the War. Thousands of men were enlisting. Woodlawn, another Bronx club, played one recorded game on Oct. 9, 1861, losing to the Exercise Club of Brooklyn 23 – 8.

Pelham had a bevy of teams: 1884 – The Muffins of City Island, Beldenites of City Island; Rivals of City Island, the

Pelhamville Nine. According to *The Chronicle* of Mt. Vernon June 18, 1889 pg.2, col.2, the Shamrocks of City Island, was 'composed of yacht men under the management of John F. Ahmuty'... 'on July 4th, the Shamrocks played the Nationals of Willet's Point,' Bronxville. [It is surprising to me that City Island, which is a narrow strip of land, barely a mile and a half long and half a mile wide, could produce so many baseball clubs in 1884]. These are just fragments, with no box scores or lists of players. Some references report one of the earliest games in Pelham was played by City Island – (*The Chronicle,* Mt. Vernon, NY, Sept 28, 1877, pg.1, col.6). Other sources were from the *New Rochelle Pioneer*, July 14, 1894 in their column entitled 'Along the Sound,' page 2, col. 3 – 'A new Base Ball club was organized [named] the Pelham Base Ball Club, under the management of T.J. Jordan of the Pelham House. Its batteries are Joseph Smith and William Barton. They secured the grounds on Locust Point and will play all uniformed clubs.' Once again there is scant information regarding the origins and statistics of these clubs.

Some of these clubs went on the road to spread the game. These tournaments, often connected with county fairs, and increased newspaper coverage gave the game new momentum after the Civil War, and what had been friendly sociable matches became serious contests, sometimes marred by bad blood. Enclosed grounds changed the nature of the game-- most notably with respect to home runs--and allowed teams to charge admission, which introduced a new element of commercialism, community involvement, and a heightened sense of competition. Ultimately, it brought about a level of play that made the best "amateur" clubs able to challenge professional teams from the East when they toured the country.

The Unions played their first match of the 1867 season with a team called the Atlanta Club of Tremont, on Saturday May 18th. They trounced the Tremont club 48 – 10, Birdsall was the winning pitcher for the Unions. [11]

UNION
Smith, ss
Abrams, rf
Pabor, lf
Martin, 2b
Akin, c
Birdsall, p
Ketchum, 2b
Austin, cf
Goldie, 1b

ATLANTA OF TREMONT
F. Purroy, ss
Miliken, rf
H. Purroy, p
Hard, lf
Jarvis, 1b
Pattison, 3b
Summerfield, 2b
Lent, cf
Sterns, c

Atlanta of Tremont Base Ball Club, won-lost record:

5/18/1867 lost to the Unions of Morrisania 48 – 10
(no date) lost to the Oriental Club of Greenpoint, NY 18 – 9

7/30/1867 lost to the Una Club of Mt. Vernon, NY 51 – 20

9/12/1867 lost to the Oriental Club of Greenpoint, NY 26 – 17

9/21/1867 lost to the Independent Club of Brooklyn, NY 48 – 12

Source: Wright, Marshall D., *The National Association of Base Ball Players, 1857 – 1870* (1998) McFarland & Company, Inc., Publishers

There was an announcement the week prior to this game in the *N.Y. Times* sports page:

> The celebrated Union Club will play its first match on Saturday next at Morrisania. The Atlanta Club of Tremont will meet the Unions on that day, and an interesting game will be the result. WATERMAN of the Mutuals, has joined the Unions, but will not play till June.
>
> - *New York Times*, May 13, 1867

BASE BALL AT
ST. JOHN'S COLLEGE

There was also a first in American intercollegiate baseball which proudly occurred in the Bronx. Fordham University in the nineteenth century was known as St. John's College, occupying the same location it does today – Fordham Road and Third Avenue. St. John's began playing baseball September 13th 1859 under the New York Rules, standardized by the NABBP the year before. The Rose Hills Base Ball Club, as they were called, played the first public game against their rivals, the College of St. Francis Xavier of Manhattan on November 11, 1859 at Fordham. This is apparently the earliest intercollegiate game played by the New York rules. According to a letter in the Walsh Library Archives of Fordham it was the first college game in the United States with nine men on each side. The Rose Hills won 33 – 11, launching an astonishing record of victories. Over the years Fordham baseball teams have won over 4,000 games, more than any other Division One program in the country. The team had no losing seasons during the nineteenth century.

The personnel for that first game in November 1859 was founder and Captain Numa Samoey of New Orleans, pitcher; John J. Gaynor of Richmond, catcher also a pitcher; Nicholas Connell of New Orleans, shortstop; E. Brownson, first base; Henry Murphy, Albany, second base; William J. Sheridan, Rochester, third base; James J. Doherty of New York, right field; James J. Sullivan, Brooklyn, left field; and Oliver McKeon of Fordham, center field. Although the game was finished in six innings, there is no indication it did not go to the full nine innings, so many records have been lost over the century.

The Rose Hills Base Ball Club of St. John's College (Fordham University), 1875. The letters on their jerseys are RH for Rose Hills (This is the earliest known photo of a campus team).

There was a further account from the University Archives that either in 1859 or 1860, a "Fordham Base-Ball team, known as the Rose Hills, captained by the late Frank Oliver, Father of present day prominent 1st alumnus, F.V.S. Oliver, defeated the famous Atlantics of Brooklyn on the front lawn of Fordham, after the Atlantics had defeated the Mutuals in the best out of five games for the Championship of the United States..." [12]

Won – Lost Record, the first ten years of St. John's (Fordham) baseball:

1859 – '60	22 – 5
1860 – '61	28 – 7
1861 – '62	26 – 8
1862 – '63	25 – 7
1863 – '64	23 – 7
1864 – '65	25 – 8
1865 – '66	26 – 9
1866 – '67	29 – 9
1867 – '68	28 – 7
1868 – '69	27 – 9
1869 – '70	28 – 8

Most baseball games were played in late March, all of April, all of May and some in early June. Besides the regular college competition, games were also played with army organizations, various athletic clubs; YMCA.'s and semi-pros. Complete records from those early years are incomplete and unavailable. In some years the editions of the record books were ready for printing before the season ended. But generally, the compilations are pretty accurate.

A majority of alumni from St. Johns College served on both sides during the Civil War. There were still a very small number of graduates, with less than one hundred bachelor's degrees from the school's inception. Out of this number, there were four generals, seven colonels, and seven captains from Fordham who served in the Union Army. Eight alumni served on the Confederate side and many others who served as privates and drummer boys. A majority of students on the

Rose Hill campus were not college students, but preparatory students in their Second and Third Divisions.

These young men living in the mid-nineteenth century were just as interested in extra-curricular activity as their counterparts are today. Many joined the baseball team. They also created a hand-written monthly literary publication, the *Goose Quill* (1853). In athletics, the first baseball team formed was the Rose Hill baseball Club in 1859 (St. John's was properly known as Rose Hill College). As mentioned earlier, the first intercollegiate game against St. Francis Xavier College of Manhattan on November 3, 1859. Through the years other teams followed: The Rose Hills, College Varsity; the Live Oaks, Second Division; which became the Invincibles in 1862, then evolved into the Fordham Prep Varsity in 1904; the Actives, a second tem to the Invincibles; and finally the Tyros, a Third Division for younger boys, actually 7th graders. The Second Division (high school) Live Oaks were a very successful team routing their opponents in every game they played. Fordham produced some of the best collegiate teams in their respective divisions. [13]

A further word about Esteban "Steve" Bellan (Class of 1866): Many of the people of Cuba had a strong resentment about Spanish colonial rule. Esteban's parents decided to send their son the New York instead of Madrid for a higher education. The 14 year old Esteban was enrolled in the Second Division, the Prep school, at St' John's in 1863. He was awarded a "Proficiency," or what was called 'first honors,' or 'high honors.' Besides excelling in his studies, he also proved himself on the baseball team. By 1866, Esteban had joined the varsity, the Rose Hills, as catcher and lead-off batter. In a game on June 1866 with an amateur team that was part of the NABBP, he had four hits, scored twice, impressing the umpire, who, as it turns out was an infielder for the Morrisania Unions. Eleven days later, Esteban along with another teammate, joined the Unions. He helped the Unions win the championship for the 1868 season. Interestingly, the policy of the NABBP was against any "colored" person playing in the Association. Esteban's mother was Irish, and so they never questioned his background. His teammates made sure of that distinction by calling him "Steve."

By 1869, he left the Unions and journeyed upstate to join the Troy Haymakers. The team became a professional club in the National Association of Professional Base Ball Players (NAPBBP) organized in 1871. Esteban was the first Latin American to play professional ball in America. His success on the field earned him the nickname, "The Cuban Sylph." [A Sylph was an elemental being in the theory of Paracelsus that inhabits air, slender and graceful]. He certainly had elegance and speed on the field. During the 1871 season he played in all 29 of the Haymaker's games with 32 hits, three doubles, three triples, and 1 .250 batting average. He caught the hottest line drives and had an accurate arm. This was in the age of barehanded baseball.

He left the Haymakers after the 1872 season and joined up with the notorious New York Mutuals. By 1874 he became a naturalized American citizen. Soon afterwards, he travelled back to Cuban and discovered baseball in his old country had become politicized. Captain General of Cuba, Francisco de Lersundi, outlawed the game in 1868. He claimed it was an "anti-Spanish game with insurrection tendencies." The

Spanish overlords preferred that the Cubans maintain their sport as bullfighting. But the people fell in love with the game and thought of it as a modern sport with the need for concentration and skill and could be watched by women and children. It was certainly different than the blood-sport of bullfighting. Since the game appealed to the people and aggravated the Spanish rulers, they adopted it wholeheartedly.

Bellan didn't return to the States, he stayed in Cuba and served as a player/manager for the newly formed baseball team, Club Habana. He played and managed in the fhe first professional baseball game at Palmar del Junco field, on December 7, 1874. His team beat the Club Matanzas 51-9. A rather convincing victory.

In 1875, two other Cubans who attended Fordham were the brothers Teodoro and Carlos De Zaldo, who undoubtedly played on the Rose Hills, founded the Almendares Club. They became the number one rivals of the Club Habana. This heated rivalry no doubt piqued interest in baseball throughout Central and South America. By the turn of the twentieth century baseball was established in Venezuela, Yucatan, Puerto Rico, and the Dominican Republic. Fordham produced those early players who had a definite influence in the spread of the game in Latin America.

Esteban continued to play baseball until he retired from the Club Habana in 1886. His legacy was a long and rich one. He was credited with being the first to hit three home runs in one game. He led his team to three championships, and has been called, "The Father of Cuban Baseball." In 1911, a statue was erected to him in Havana. He died in Cuba on August 8, 1932.

He was inducted into the Fordham Hall of Fame in 1989 and featured in an exhibit at the DiMenna Children's Museum at the New York Historical Society. [14]

Rose Hills Base Ball Club (Fordham, N.Y.)

10/27/1864 lost to the Active Club, NY 32 – 16
06/18/1868 defeated the Active Club, NY 36 – 34
06/03/1869 lost to the Eckford Club, Bklyn 10 – 6
07/01/1869 lost to the Eckford Club, Bklyn 34 – 14
10/14/1869 lost to the Mutuals, NY, 11 – 10

1870

05/05 lost to the Union of Morrisania 16 – 10
05/26 lost to the Mutuals, NY 21 – 6
06/01 defeated Yale, New Haven, Connecticut 19 – 13
06/02 lost to the Union of Morrisania 35 – 8
07/01 lost to the Mutuals, NY 27 - 18
07/02 defeated the Alpha Club of Brooklyn 15 – 7
07/05 lost to Harvard, Cambridge, Massachusetts 17 – 2
10/18 lost to Princeton, Princeton, New Jersey 22 – 18
11/17 defeated the Alert Club, NY 34 – 22

Rose Hills Roster

1870

McManus, 1b
McDermott, 2b
Tremp, ss
W. Gallagher, 3b, of
Dooley, of
Gleavy, of, 3b, c
Swayne, of, 1b
Villa, c
Burns, p

Source: Wright, Marshall D., *The National Association of Base Ball Players, 1857-1870,* 2000 McFarland & Co., Publishers

AFTERWORD

For most baseball fans the history of the game is a combination of remembered feelings and the facts. Those memories can form a deep reservoir of feeling and we treat it with the utmost seriousness. To the fan, this is 'not just a game.' It is a microcosm of life itself, with all its thrills and boredom. We have made an emotional investment here and we want it to pay off. The spectator has a relationship with the participants and vice versa. And this has been true throughout the history of the game. That is why the connection to the past is cemented to the present. So many of the controversies of modern baseball can find its roots in the past. They are similar and repetitious. We can all recognize those disputes and we have a deep understanding of them. Intense and remarkably similar emotions are regularly sparked by a game of baseball. This why the games are remembered and experienced so intensely. We feel the same excitement, fears, and ambivalence that were felt by the generations that preceded us.

From one generation to the next, there is always that claim, "somehow or other they don't play ball nowadays as they used to some eight or ten years ago…they don't play with the same kinds of feelings or for the same object(ives) they used to." This is an excerpt from a veteran player's letter dated Jan. 9, 1868. It could just as well have been written today.

Baseball was an urban game that spread nationwide into the rural backwaters. What started as an amateur endeavor, by mid-1870s had become a substantial commercial undertaking. What was originally in the 1850s a club-based fraternal sport, within two decades turned into a business, an entertainment business, not a recreation requiring a front office, management, a board of directors, gate receipts and paid labor of its ballplayers and coaches. The 'reserve clause' introduced in 1879 was designed to eliminate players' freedom in the marketplace and thereby permanently put a cap on their salaries. The ballplayers became chattel, property of the owners, to be traded and fired at the owners' whim. The owners got wealthy, while the players struggled to sustain themselves on a paltry salary and unpaid 'bonuses.' It wasn't until Curt Flood sued Commissioner Bowie Kuhn and Major League Baseball to win free agency and finally abolish the reserve clause. Some would argue this paved the way for exorbitant salaries and the dilution of the game because of market share problems and the plethora of teams and the sacrilege of inter-league play during the regular season. Even the DH has had its moments. But baseball has survived the scandals, the anti-trust suits, the corruption and other events that shocked the game over the last hundred and fifty years.

Even though baseball has undergone enormous changes in its scale and organization it has survived and prospered. Here again, the reasons are clear. Fans and players have the same experiences their forbearers had a century and a half ago. There is no gulf to leap across, the modern fan and the crank of 1868 would immediately forge a bond and recognize what the other was feeling about this glorious game of baseball.

Even those who report the game have an affinity with their brother newspaper men of the past. Some played the game (we all have played to a certain extent if only in our childhood and adolescence). The early writers and reporters participated in club social affairs, accompanied the clubs on their tours of other cities, and got involved in club politics. They had a vested interest in how their team represented their city. These reporters sat in a special position between the players and the spectators on the field, at a table which came to be known by the early 1860s as the "press box." How interesting that the terms of the past are still used today. Even our day-to-day speech is laced with baseball references: 'right off the bat,' 'touching base,' 'you hit a home run,' 'threw him a curve,' and hundreds of other distinctive usages of baseball jargon. In the language of baseball no other sport has contributed more words to American English than baseball. *The Dickson Baseball Dictionary* (2009) covers more than ten thousand terms. Baseball is deeply imbedded in our society and culture.

Bart Giamatti once observed: "It has long been my conviction that we can learn far more about the conditions, and values, of a society by contemplating how it chooses to play, to use its free time, to take its leisure, than by examining how it goes about its work." From, *Take Time for Paradise* (1989).

And Jacques Barzun's sums it up in his renowned claim that, "Whoever wants to know the heart and mind of America had better learn baseball."

Over time, we have come to know the true nature of baseball. It is not the laconic rural pastime many assume characterized the nineteenth century game. It was graceful, vibrant, constantly developing and gaining in popularity and maturity. The Yankees, for example, are a franchise that has reached the zenith of success, but it was those teams that came before that have paved the way for the game we know and love today. Baseball in the Bronx has a long and rich history, and is part of baseball's family tree. The teams that played there served an integral role in contributing to the origins, evolution and spread of the game throughout the nation. Further research will discover more information on the teams and their legacy will be added to the story. As time goes on an even more detailed picture will emerge. The people of the Bronx can take special pride in that legacy and history.

FOOTNOTES

[1] *Brooklyn Daily Eagle,* Sunday, July 19, 1891 "Chapter 6:13 of the laws of 1873 of the state of New York, provide: for the taking of Morrisania, West Farms and Kingsbridge from Westchester County and adding them to New York city and county."

[2] **New York's Great Fire of 1835** destroyed much of lower Manhattan on a December night so frigid that volunteer firemen were unable to battle the walls of flame as water froze in their hand-pumped fire engines. Most of the present day financial district of New York City was reduced to smoking rubble.

[3] These men were listed as the first officers of the Unions by Wm. Sutton's son, T. Emery Sutton, (born 1859). He was living at 430 East 160th Street, Bronx at the time of his interview with reporter William Wood, on Aug. 18, 1938. *'Old Morrisania Town,'* Library of Congress, "American Life Histories: Manuscript from the Federal Writers' Project, 1936-1940." However, *The New York Herald*, July 21, 1855, recorded a rather different list: Thomas E. Sutton, President; Henry Brandow, Vice President; William Cauldwell, Secretary; James Parshall, Treasurer; and Thomas Greener, Game Keeper. This is an example of how early sources conflict. Researchers and scholars are left to find new resources and sift through available documents to get at the facts.

[4] *Brooklyn Daily Eagle,* Thursday, Sep. 8, 1898, pg 11

[5] *Brooklyn Daily Eagle*, Monday, July 28, 1862 pg 2

[6] Wright, Marshall D., "The National Association of Base Ball Players, 1857 – 1870." (2000, McFarland & Company, Inc., Publishers, Jefferson, NC)

[7] *Brooklyn Daily Eagle*, Monday, Oct. 5, 1868. A reference to the Unions field in Tremont appears in the announcement of the championship game to be played the next day between the visiting Atlantics and The Union club:

> **"THE GAME TO-MORROW** – To-morrow the Atlantics go to Morrisania or rather Tremont to play the return game between the two clubs. In view of the fact that the Atlantics are determined to win it if possible, it is reasonable to presume they will. If they do there is no doubt that they will bring back with them the championship, consequently they will receive the gold ball from Frank Queen.* A very large crowd is expected to attend the match. To accommodate it the Harlem Railroad will run a special train in time to reach the ground. To accommodate the Brooklyn folks the steamer Sylvan Shore will start from Fulton Ferry at half past twelve o'clock connecting with the Fordham avenue cars, for the Union ground. Returning leave Mott Haven at 6:30 P.M. at the arrival of the cars from the ball ground."

*Frank Queen was the founder and editor of the *New York Clipper*.

[8] *Brooklyn Daily Eagle*, Wed. Sept, 9, 1868 pg 2. "Bearman joins Unions…" There was also a rather worrisome article entitled "Where are our players of another generation to

come from?" The editors seemed concerned about the gradual encroachment of commercial and residential development destroying the playing fields of the clubs.

> "...gradual building upon the vacant lots in the city [of Brooklyn], those spots which were the nurseries of the ball players; those places that made Brooklyn the reputation of making the best ball players, have driven the boys from the old grounds..."

This was also true throughout Manhattan and the Bronx, as evidenced by Morrisania abandoning Melrose Station to relocate further north to Tremont and Arthur Avenues.

[9] *New York Sunday Mercury*, Sep. 20, 1856

[10] *Newark Daily Advertiser*, Aug. 30, 1860

[11] *Brooklyn Daily Eagle*, Monday, May 20, 1867 "The Unions played their first match of the season on their grounds, with the Atlanta Club, of Tremont..."

[12] "All Time Baseball Records" – Fordham University Archives *"Fordham Baseball Notes,"* Surveys made from May 1956 through June 1958.

[13] Holbrook, Francis X. and Stellwag, August A., *When September Comes: A History of Fordham Preparatory School, 1841 – 1991*, New York, The Seven Graphic Arts, Inc., 1990, pp.15 and 18.

[14] *Fordham Preparatory School Hall of Honor Introduction Dinner Journal*, Botanical Garden, The Bronx, NY, November 18, 2011, p. 5-6

A BRIEF CHRONOLOGY OF THE EARLY GAME

(With Rule Changes During the Amateur Era)

1842 New York Nine is organized.

1843   New York Knickerbockers organized. [Before the Knickerbockers, variants of the rules were played all over the country. Regions developed their own bat-and-ball games.]

1845 – 1846 Knicks formerly adopt rules. [Note: the Knickerbockers didn't invent the game; they reinvented it by transforming a child's game into a 'grownup' game with an adult's seriousness of purpose].

1850 - Five years later, the Knicks draw up the ancestor of today's rules, the N.Y. Rules adopted by the Washington Club of New York(1851)

1853 - 1854 Tenuous existence of multiple clubs around New York. The Gotham, Eagle and Active Clubs.

1853 - *N.Y. Sunday Mercury* under Wm. Cauldwell begins publication of game accounts.

1855 - The Union of Morrisania is organized.

1856 - Manly Virtues of Base Ball Extolled; 25 Clubs Now Playing in NYC Area

"The game of Base Ball is one, when well played, that requires strong bones, tough muscle, and sound mind; and no athletic game is better calculated to strengthen the frame and develop a full, broad chest, testing a man's powers of endurance most severely . . . "I have no doubt that some twenty-five Clubs . . . could be reckoned up within a mile or two of New-York, that stronghold of 'enervated' young men." "Base Ball" [letter to the editor], *New York Times*, September 27, 1856. Full text is reprinted in Dean A. Sullivan, Compiler and Editor, <u>Early Innings: A Documentary History of Baseball, 1825-1908</u> [University of Nebraska Press, 1995], pp. 21-22.

1856 - *New York Mercury, and the NY Clipper* Term Base Ball the "National Pastime"

The New York Mercury refers to base ball as "The National Pastime." Letter to the editor from "a baseball lover," The letter was reprinted as a part of the long article, "Base Ball, Cricket, and Skating," *Spirit of the Times*, Volume 1, number 16 (December 20, 1856), pp. 260 - 261. This is perhaps the earliest appearance of the term "national pastime" to denote base ball.

1857- 1858 National Association of Base Ball Players (NABBP) the game's first governing body is founded. Sixteen charter member clubs including the Morrisania Unions. The New York Rules, the precursor to modern day baseball, are adopted. The game was won when one side scored 21 "aces,"

Now, it is a nine inning contest with the highest scoring team winning.

> William H. van Cott is elected NABBP President. "Our National Sports," *Porter's Spirit of the Times*, January 31, 1857. Reprinted in Dean A. Sullivan, Compiler and Editor, <u>Early Innings: A Documentary History of Baseball, 1825-1908</u> [University of Nebraska Press, 1995], pp. 22-24. Peter Morris notes that the NABBP commissioned five men "to confer with the Central Park Commissioners in relation to a grant of public lands for base ball purposes." Morris, Peter, <u>Level Playing Fields: How the Groundskeeping Murphy Brothers Shaped Baseball</u> (University of Nebraska Press, 2007), page 18

1857 - Rules Modified to Specify Nine Innings, 90-Foot Base Paths, Nine-Player Teams

> "The New York Game rules are modified by a group of 16 clubs who send representatives to meetings to discuss the conduct of the New York Game. The Knickerbocker Club recommends that a winner be declared after seven innings but nine innings are adopted instead upon the motion of Lewis F. Wadsworth. The base paths are fixed by D.L. Adams at 30 yards - the old rule had specified 30 paces and the pitching distance at 15 yards. Team size is set at nine players." The convention decided not to eliminate bound outs, but did give fly outs more weight by requiring runners to return to their bases after fly outs.

<u>Spirit of the Times</u>, January 31, 1857. Reprinted in Dean A. Sullivan, Compiler and Editor, <u>Early Innings: A Documentary History of Baseball, 1825-1908</u> [University of Nebraska Press, 1995], pp. 122-24. For a full account of the convention, see Frederick Ivor-Campbell, "Knickerbocker Base Ball: The Birth and Infancy of the Modern Game," <u>Base Ball</u>, Volume 1, Number 2 (Fall 2007), pages 55-65.

Roger Adams writes that the terms "runs" and "innings" first appear in the 1857 rules, as well as the first specifications of the size and weight of the base ball. R. Adams, "Nestor of Ball Players," found in typescript in the Chadwick Scrapbooks.

1858 – 1859 The game spreads. Called strikes are introduced. A batter is out when a ball, fair or foul, is caught on a fly or one bounce.

1858 - Base Ball Sheet Music Appears

Blodgett, J. (composer), "The Base Ball Polka" [Buffalo, Blodgett and Bradford], per David Block, <u>Baseball Before We Knew It</u>, page 218. Block marks this as the first baseball sheet music, as composed by a member of the Niagara Base Ball Club of Buffalo. "On the title page, under an emblem of two crossed bats over a baseball, is a dedication "To the Flour City B. B. Club of Rochester, N.Y. by the Niagara B. B. Club.'"

1858 - New York All-Stars Beat Brooklyn All-Stars, 2 games to 1; First Admission Fees Are Charged

"The Great Base Ball Match of 1858, which was a best 2 out of 3 games series, embodies four landmark events that are pivotal to the game's history" 1. It was organized base ball's very first all-star game. 2. It was the first base ball game in the New York metropolitan area to be played on an enclosed ground. 3. It marked the first time that spectators paid for the privilege of attending a base ball game. 4. The game played on September 10, 1858 is at present the earliest known instance of an umpire calling strike on a batter." Schaefer, Robert H., "The Great Base Ball Match of 1858: Base Ball's First All-Star Game," *Nine,* Volume 14, no 1, (2005), pp 47-66. Coverage of the game in *Porter's Spirit of the Times*, July 24, 1858, is reprinted in Dean A. Sullivan, Compiler and Editor, Early Innings: A Documentary History of Baseball, 1825-1908 [University of Nebraska Press, 1995], pp. 27-29. The *Spirit of the Times* article itself is "The Great Base Ball Match," *Spirit of the Times,* Volume 28, number 24

1858 - NY Game Rules Changed - The Called Strike used

The New York Game adopts the called strike, first employed at a New York vs. Brooklyn all-star game at Fashion Race Course on Long Island. The umpire to call the first strike is D.L. Adams. The National Association of Base Ball Players' rules are in <u>Constitution and By-laws of the NABBP</u> [New York, Wilbur and Hastings, 1859], per David Block, <u>Baseball Before We Knew It</u>, page 224.

1859 – The Rose Hills Base Ball Club of St. John's is organized under New York Rules.

1859 – First Intercollegiate Game [First Played by the New York Rules] St. John's (Fordham) vs. Xavier.

Sullivan, Dean A., Compiler and Editor, Early Innings: A Documentary History of Baseball, 1825 – 1908 [University of Nebraska Press, 1995], p. 32. Sullivan dates the game November 3, 1859, but does not give a source.

1859 - New Yorker Dies Playing Base Ball

"Yesterday afternoon, THOMAS WILLIS, a young man, residing at No. 46 Greenwich-street, met with a sad accident while playing ball in the Elysian Fields, Hoboken. Acting in the capacity of "fielder" he ran after the ball, which rolled into a hole about fifteen feet deep. Slipping and falling in his eagerness to obtain it, his head struck a sharp rock, which fractured his skull. Medical attendance was immediately procured, but the injury was pronounced fatal." *New York Evening Express*, October 22, 1859, page 3 column 3. Perhaps the first fatality recorded before Jim Creighton's death in 1862.

1859 - Annual Meeting of NABBP Decides: Bound Rule Retained, Fly Rule Voted Down

"Base Ball," *The New York Clipper* (March 26, 1859). The fly rule lost by a 32-30 vote, and the paper worried that easy fielding would "reduce the 'batting' part of the game to a nonentity. Compensation for playing any game was outlawed. The official ball shrunk slightly in weight and size. Matches would be decided by single games.

1859 - *Morning Express* Opposes Bound Rule, Tag-up Rule: Wants More Runs!

Reporting on the upcoming Knicks-Excelsiors game: "We believe that the rule, which is allowed by the Convention, of putting a man out, if the ball is caught on the first bound, is to be laid aside in this match. The more manly game of taking the ball on the fly, is alone to be retained. ... We do not know whether the men are to return to their bases in the event of a ball being caught on the fly; but it appears to us, that it would be as fair to one team as the other if the bases could be retained, if made before the ball had got to there, [and] it would cause more runs to be made, and a much more lively and satisfactory game." *New York Morning_Express* (June 30, 1859), page 3, column 6. Posted to 19CBB by George Thompson, 3/18/2007. A fortnight later, a return match "in the test game of catching the ball on the fly" was scheduled for August 2, 1859: "Knickerbocker vs. Excelsior," *New York Morning Post* (July 13, 1859), page 3, column 7. A long inning-by-inning game account appears at

New York Morning Express (August 3, 1859), page 3, column 7.

1860 - NABBP Refines Rules on the Ball

For the third year, the Convention put the elimination of the bound rule to a vote, and again the bound rule won, 55-37. The Association's own Rules and Regulations Committee, chaired by Doc Adams, had favored a move to the fly rule for fair balls. Membership had reached nearly 80 clubs from as far away as Michigan. New York Herald, 3/18/1860.

The National Association of Baseball Players rules now specify that "The ball must weigh not less than five and three-fourths, nor more than six ounces avoirdupois. It must measure not less than nine and three-fourths, nor more than ten inches in circumference. It must be composed of India rubber and yarn, and covered with leather, and, in all match games, shall be furnished by the challenging club, and become the property of the winning club, as a trophy of victory." 1860 National Association of Baseball Players, Rules and Regulations Adopted by the National Association of Baseball Players - New York, March 14th 1860.

1860 - Chadwick's Beadle's Appears, and the Baseball Press is Launched

Chadwick, Henry, Beadle's Dime Base-Ball Player: A Compendium of the Game, Comprising Elementary

Instructions of the American Game of Base Ball [New York, Irwin P. Beadle] per David Block, *Baseball Before We Knew It*, page 221. The first annual baseball guide, emblematic, perhaps, of the transformation of base ball into a spectator sport. The 40-page guide includes rules for Knickerbocker ball, the new NABBP rules, rules for the Massachusetts game, and for rounders. Chadwick includes a brief history of base ball, saying it is of "English origin" and "derived from rounders." Block observes: "For twenty-five years his pronouncements remained the accepted definition of the game's origins. Then the controversy erupted. First John Montgomery Ward and then Albert Spalding attacked Chadwick's theory. Ultimately, their jingoistic efforts saddled the nation with the Doubleday Myth."

1861 – 1865 The Civil War slows growth and ends careers of many clubs and ballplayers.

1861, December 11 - The 5th annual convention of the National Association of Base Ball Players is held at Clinton Hall in New York, but the War cuts the attendance down to 34 delegates. This number won't be topped until 1865

1863 - Bat size is regulated. The pitcher's box is now 12' x 4'. The pitcher must have both feet on the ground when pitching. He can no longer take a step during his delivery. Home base and the pitcher's box must be marked. No base can be made on a foul ball.

1864, December 14 - The 8th annual meeting of the National Association of Base Ball Players is held at Clinton

Hall with 30 clubs in attendance. The rules committee recommends adoption of the "fly game," making bounced outs in fair territory illegal and it will be adopted for next season as the "regular" game. Base runners must touch each base while making the circuit. Henry Chadwick's scoring system is introduced and adopted.

1865, December 13 -. The 9th convention of the National Association of Base Ball Players is held at Cooper Union. There are 90 clubs represented there, three times last year's attendance. Batting averages are included in the statistics

1866 - 1867 Great boom of baseball enthusiasm.

1866, June 16 - At Morrisania, the Union Club defeated the Enterprise Club of Brooklyn by the score of 42-16. The Unions led all the way and, according to the *New York Times,* "did some tall batting after the third inning. The fielding of the Enterprise nine was very loose, while the Unions, although, they were short Abrams at third and Austin at right, fielded very well. The attendance was quite large, the belles of Morrisania gracing the scene with their presence in unusual numbers. At the conclusion of the game the Brooklyn boys were nicely entertained by the victors."

1866, December 12 - The 10th annual convention of the National Association of Base Ball Players is held at Clinton Hall in New York City with a record 202 clubs sending delegates. Rule changes include the introduction of called balls, after a warning from the umpire, with 3 called balls allowing the batter to first base. This session introduces the pitcher's box, an area 6 feet wide and 4 feet deep, from which the pitcher must deliver the ball.

1867, October 10 - The Union Club of Morrisania takes the 1867 Championship, winning their 2nd game of the series, 14-13, over the Atlantics. Charley Pabor is the winning pitcher.

1867, December 9 - The NABBP bans blacks "on political grounds." The Nominating Committee, in issuing a blanket acceptance of new applicants, states that, "It is not presumed by your committee that any club who have applied are composed of persons of color, or any portion of them; and the recommendations of our committee in this report are based upon this view, and they unanimously report against the admission of any club which may be composed of one or more colored persons." The Base Ball Chronicle of December 19 reports that "the report of the Nominating Committee... was presented, the feature of it being there commendation to exclude colored clubs from representation in the Association, the object being to keep out of the Convention the discussion of any subject having a political bearing, as this undoubtedly had." The pitcher's box is now made into a 6 foot square and the pitcher is permitted to move around inside the box. The batter is given the privilege of calling for a high or low pitch.

1868, December 9 – The 12th annual convention of the NABBP was held in Washington, DC. A new rule states that "no game shall be considered as played unless 5 innings on each side have been completed." The National Association decided to divide the players into classes, and for the first time recognizes professionals. This officially marks the end of the amateur era.

1869 - Professional play common.

1870, March 27 - In a letter to the editor published in today's *New York Sunday Mercury,* Cincinnati Red Stockings' manager Harry Wright writes about hand signals, "There is one thing I would like to see the umpire do at (a) big game, and that is, raise his hand when a man is out. You know what noise there is always when a fine play is made on the bases, and it being impossible to hear the umpire, it is always some little time before the player knows whether he is given out or not. It would very often save a great deal of bother and confusion." Interesting account suggesting that the use of hand signals was being considered long before "Dummy" Hoy introduced them in 1887.

1870, November 30 - The 14th annual convention of the NABBP was held in New York, the attendance of delegates being smaller than any previous convention. William Wansley, Ed Duffy, and Thomas Devyr are reinstated to professional baseball, and William H. Craver is expelled for dishonorable play. Rule changes include allowing the batter to overrun first base after touching it.

1871, March 17 – The National Association of Professional Baseball Players was formed in New York at a convention called together by Henry Chadwick. The meeting was held at Collier's Saloon on the corner of 13th Street and Broadway. Playing rules are same as the amateur players' with the exception of player compensation. Each club will play 5 games with the other clubs and the winner of 3 will have won that championship series. The league championship will be awarded to the team winning the most series against the other teams and not on a total wins or percentage basis as would be done in later years. Teams represented at the convention are: Athletics of Philadelphia, Boston Red Stockings (who hired Harry Wright), to represent them after the Cincinnati Reds disbanded), Chicago White Stockings, Eckford of Brooklyn, Forest City of Cleveland, Forest Citys of Rockford, IL, Mutuals of New York, Nationals of Washington, DC, Olympics of Washington, and the Union Club of Troy, NY, known as the Haymakers. Teams not present but playing matches in the first season of the National Association are the Atlantics of Brooklyn and the Kekiongas of Fort Wayne, IN. The Union of Morrisania refuses to enroll.

1872, March 4 - The National Association of Professional Baseball Players holds its annual convention in Cleveland. Eight clubs send delegates. Bob Ferguson, Atlantics, is elected president. Each team is required to play a series of 5 games with each club. Whoever wins the most games will be declared champion. The rules will now permit the use of the wrist in pitching. Ball size and weight are regulated and remain the same to the present day

1872, July 26 -The National Association holds a special meeting, resolving that, because some teams have dropped out of the race for 1872 (Troy, Nationals, and Olympics), 9 games will be played between contending teams this season instead of 5.

1873, March 13 - Delegates from the existing professional clubs of the country assemble in Baltimore to establish a permanent Professional Association. Teams represented are the Athletics, Atlantics, Baltimores, Boston Reds, Marylands of Baltimore, Resolute of New Jersey, and the Washingtons. A constitution is adopted along with Henry Chadwick's code of rules. For the first time a uniform ball (Ryan's dead ball) must be used in all games

1873 – Morrisania Unions disbanded.

APPENDIX I

These newspaper accounts will give the reader a flavor of what it was like living in mid-nineteenth century New York. How the games were played, commentary, period ads, real estate values at Morrisania in particular.

• *New-York Daily Tribune*, November 6, 1850: **"Morrisania land for sale"** – About 16 acres of Land, eligibly for building lots, lying on the Old Boston Turnpike or Morse Avenue and within about 5 minutes walk of the Harlem Railroad Depot. The land is high and wooded, and streets are already opened around it. Apply for a few days in person, to W.E. ROBINSON, 304 B'way Room 26, 2d floor between the hours of 10 A.M. and 12 P.M. or by letter, at the Tribune office.   h2 1w

• *New York Tribune*, April 27, 1852 pg 3: Mrs. Jerrard's Boarding School for Young ladies, at Morrisania, Village of Morrisania within an hour's ride by the Harlem railway, from City Hall. Circulars obtained from Lewis Colby No. 122 Nassau St.

• *New-York Daily Tribune*, July 27, 1852, pg.1, col. 6 – real estate advertisement:

East Morrisania Village – About 360 Lots, varying in size from eighth of an acre to six acres, are now offered for sale on the most favorable terms. Ten percent down, and balance on or before March 1854. These lots occupy a very healthy and beautiful location near and in full view of the East River, and in the immediate vicinity of the grounds and residences of several of the most wealthy and respectable citizens of Westchester County. This village is connected with the Harlem Railroad by a branch Railroad. For maps and other information apply to D.B. WINTON, No. 5 Tryon-row near Harlem Railroad Office, opposite City Hall.

• October 14th, 1862:

The Excelsiors defeat the Unions of Morrisania 13-9. Jim Creighton hits 4 doubles and scores 4 runs, but suffers 'an internal injury occasioned by strain' hitting a HR. Considered the premier player of the day, he dies of a ruptured bladder four days later at the age of 21.

A monument was erected at Greenwood Cemetery in Brooklyn inscribed under a wreath: "James Creighton, son of James and Jane Creighton, April 15, 1841; Oct 18, 1862" A baseball was fashioned in stone that rest atop the uppermost pinnacle of the tall stone monument. Lengthy tributes appeared in many of the local newspapers and his grave became a Mecca for baseball players.

Additional sources with references to players and the Unions:

• *Brooklyn Daily Eagle*, Aug. 8, 1864, pg 2: "**UNION VS EMPIRE** – The Union Club of Morrisania will play their first game of the season at Morrisania on Thursday next, their opponent being Empires. It will be quite a nice little trip to take the Harlem boat from Harlem to Morrisnia to see this match. Hennigan plays short stop with Pinckney to pitch, Marsh and Hudson being in the Union nine."

● *Brooklyn Daily Eagle*, July 6, 1866 pg 2. The Washington Nationals visit Morrisania. The Union lineup:

> Martin, 2b; Abrams, lf; Smith, 1b; Hannegan, ss; Pabor, p; Birdsall, c; Hudson, rf; Ketchum, 3b; Austin, cf.

> Morrisania defeated the Nationals 22 – 8 in seven innings, the game called on account of rain. Time of the game: 2 hours, 20 minutes… also recorded was the umpire, scorers, runs scored, strike outs, base on balls, out on foul balls, out on bases, passed balls, strike outs, left on base, fly catches, flies missed etc. Most box scores from this period carried this information.

● *Brooklyn Daily Eagle*, June 22, 1868 pg 2: **Unions vs. Star at Capitoline Grounds** – The Union lineup includes the following players: Pabor p; Wright, 2b; Birdsall, c; Shelley, 3b; Beals, rf; Ayres, ss; Goldie, 1b; Austin, cf; Simmons, lf.

● *Brooklyn Daily Eagle,* Friday, Aug. 9, 1868, pg 2: **"Bulletin of Changes** – Christadoro and Bellan from the Rose Hill Club, to the Unions of Morrisania."

● *Brooklyn Daily Eagle*, Aug. 5, 1897, a letter was written to the editor by G. Smith Stanton, a former baseball player who played in the fifties and early sixties. He tracked down another veteran, 53 year old Charles J. Smith (Charley), 3rd baseman for the Atlantic Club of Brooklyn in those years, and recorded Smith's reminiscences. Here are excerpts from that letter:

> Great Neck, Long Island, New York, July 28, 1897
> To the editor of the Brooklyn Eagle:
>
> …"In those days the player's bench was the grass, a short distance back of the umpire. The grand stand and bleachers were also the grass – standing room only. The crowd was kept back by ropes strung a certain distance from the foul lines. The umpire was chosen by the captains of the two nines from some neutral club just before the game…"
>
> "Those were the days that tried pitchers' bodies and souls. A batsman was not obliged to strike at a ball until he got one to suit him. I once saw Hannegan of the Morrisanias pitch seventy balls to Andy Mills before Mills struck at one. Many a base ball battle was fought to a finish on the old Elysian Fields at Hoboken…Joe Start was the only first baseman who had the call over Goldie."
>
> "The great national game is indebted to those old veterans in more ways than one. In the first place there was no salary; on the contrary, there was an initiation fee and all had to pay dues and furnish their own uniforms, and pay their own travelling expenses. The consequence was different businesses they followed were neglected, and, with few exceptions, they

accumulated little of this world's goods...."

... " Loving cups are presented to and benefits given for the pioneers of other vocations, but I know of no more deserving ones than the few who are left of the old veterans, who back in the fifties sacrificed their business future, disfigured themselves for life, while contributing their skill to make popular the national game of America to-day..."

G. Smith Stanton

● *The Daily Evening Telegraph*, Philadelphia, Pennsylvania, Tuesday, August 20, 1867, pg. 4, col.2:

"The Base-Ball Excitement. – We have lately heard so little of the base-ball excitement that the dissipation caused by that game had at last died out, but it seems that it has been a smouldering (sic) fire, which has now burst forth. The Athletics of Philadelphia has gone to New York, to play against a number of the leading clubs there for the championship of America. The first day's match with the Union of Morrisania resulted in the success of the Philadelphia Club. We are heartily glad that such is the issue, as we have our local pride, and desire to see our fellow citizens triumph; at the same time, we do not feel enthusiastic on the subject of games for championship, which only engenders ill-feeling, give occasion for gambling, and cause a vast loss of time and expenditure of money, without any return either to the *physique* or *morals* of those engaged. A friendly game with neighbors without going hundreds of miles and spending hundreds of dollars, would be equally beneficial and much more sensible."

• *New-York Daily Tribune,* Thursday, November 14, 1867, pg. 5, col. 4 (Bronx Clubs in bold-face):

Base-Ball. New-York State Association.

"An adjourned meeting of the New-York State Association of Base-Ball Players was held at Masonic Hall last night. The Association, although organized only two weeks ago, already comprises the most prominent clubs in the State, and will, by the commencement of next season, probably have a majority of the whole number in its fold. The clubs represented last night were as follows: Atlantic, Brooklyn; **Atlanta, Tremont**; Athlete, Washington Highth (sic); Athletic, Brooklyn; Baltic, New-York; Cypress, East New-York; Excelsior, Brooklyn; Exercise, New-York; Excelsior, Brooklyn; Endeavor, New-York; Eagle, New-York; Eclectic, New-York; Eckford, New-York; Eagle, Brooklyn; Eagle, Flatbush; Fulton, New-York; Gotham, New-York; Gramercy, New-York; Gulick, New-York; Harlem, New-York; Harmonia, Brooklyn; Independent, Brooklyn; Jefferson, New-York; Knickerbocker, New-York; Lone Star, Matteawan; Manhattan, new-York; Marion, Brooklyn; Meteor, Addison; Mansion, New-York; Mohawk, Brooklyn; Niagara Falls; Niagara, Lockport; Nepperstein, Albany; Oriental, Greenpoint; Mutual, New-York; resolute, Brooklyn; Port Chester; Star, Brooklyn; Star, Pleasanton's; Union, Lansingburgh; **Union, Morrisania**; Staten Island; Una, Mount Vernon.

"Mr. Albro of the **Union Club of Morrisania**, was President pro. tem., and Mr. M. J. Kelley of the Gotham Club, Secretary pro. tem. The first business before the Association was the consideration of a Constitution and By-Laws... The regulations which now g(o)vern the State Association resemble, and in many cases are identical with, those of the National Association. Some wise innovations have been introduced; one of them is a clause prohibiting the playing by a club of anyone who is not an active member and has not a vote in the club...Col. J. E. Jones of the Meteor Club of Addison was as the representative of the "Southern tier," unanimously elected Second Vice President...Delegates to the National Convention, [included] Mr. Herring of the **Union Club**...One motion of the committee of five to report upon the feasibility of procuring a commodious playground in the City and County of New-York."

• *New-York Daily Tribune*, New York, [NY], September 9, 1857, page 2, col. 2 (real estate ad):

TO LET, in MORRISANIA. – Half of a comfortable double COTTAGE HOUSE, pleasantly situated on the old Boston Post Road and easy of access to the City. Call on or address M.L. No. 47 West 26th St., New York City.

• *The Charleston Daily News*, Charleston South Carolina, Friday Morning, Oct. 23, 1868, News Summary, pg. 2., col. 1:

"The International base ball match between nine of the All-England cricketers and the Union of Morrisania was played in New York on Tuesday. The Unions won by a score of 38 to 21."

• *The Charleston Daily News*, Charleston, S.C., Wednesday Morning, Oct. 28, 1868, pg. 2, col.1, News Summary"

"The last and most interesting series of base ball matches played by the English cricketers took place last Saturday, on the Union Grounds at Morrisania, New York, the occasion being testimonial to the English Cricketers by the base ball fraternity of New York. The American nine was composed of players from the Union, Mutual and Active Clubs. Six innings were played, and the game resulted in another defeat for the Britishers, the score being England, 11; America, 20."

• *The Evening Telegraph*, Philadelphia, PA, Oct. 21, 1868, Fifth Edition, pg. 3, col. 1:

"**New York, Oct. 20.** – The international base ball match between the nine of All-England Cricketers and the Union nine of Morrisania was played to-day on the St. George's cricket ground [Staten Island], the Unions winning [by] a score of 38 to 21, the Englishman (sic) accepting no odds. About 2000 people were present. The English cricketers divide and select five resident cricketers on each side, and will play a cricket match between two elevens on Wednesday and Thursday, for the benefit of the St. George professionals, **G. [George] Wright** and Norley." [Before George Wright joined the Union of Morrisania in 1866, he was a prominent cricket player and continued to play even after he became a star baseball player].

In another article below this one:

"A meeting was held to-night of capitalists who favor the construction of a canal across the Isthmus of Darien, to connect the Caribbean (sic) sea with the Pacific Ocean, at the residence of Peter Cooper, to discuss the various plans proposed."

• *The Daily Evening Telegraph*, Philadelphia, [PA], Monday, June 27, 1870:

Fifth Edition, The Latest News, Base-Ball, Athletics vs. Unions of Morrisania, Special Despatch (sic) **to the Evening Telegraph**

Seventeenth Street and Columbia Avenue, June 27. – About three thousand people are present to witness the home and home game between the champion Athletics and the Unions of Morrisania. Mr. Halbach, of the Keystones, was selected for umpire. The play commenced at 3:15, with the Unions at Bat.

First Inning

Unions – were skunked, Reynolds and Shelby going out on foul. Malone and Pabor out on fly by Bechtel.

Athletics – Reach and McBride out; Malone, Fisher and Sensenderfer got home – three runs.

Second Inning

Unions – Birdsall got home. Bass out by Reach. Austin struck out. Gedney out on fly by Pratt – one run.

Athletics – Bechtel made a home run by long hit to centre field. Reach and Malone out by Kenny, and Fisler out on fly by Austin – one run.

Third Inning

Unions – Pabor made a home run. Higham, Reynolds, and Shelly also scored. 4 runs.

Athletics – Schaffer and Radcliffe made runs.

Fourth Inning

Unions 5; Athletics 7

[The game was still in progress when the newspaper went to press. The final score was Athletics 51, Unions 20].

"Be the decisions of an Umpire what they may, they should be silently received and abided by to the end of time." – *The Clipper*. 1859. The umpire stood cool, aloof, and impartial.

• *New-York Daily Tribune*, November 6, 1850, pg 6, col. 5:

Morrisania Village. – For Sale, that beautiful portion of the BATHGATE FARM lying upon the Harlem Railroad and connecting the villages of Upper and Lower Morrisania, thus forming the central part of one village, extending over to miles upon the line of the said railroad. This property has been surveyed and laid out into building-lots, continuing from 4 to

3 ordinary city lots each with convenient streets and avenues and will be disposed of upon the same plan as the tract which now comprises the village of Morrisania. Books are now open at 455 Broadway, and the hotel, Morrisania village, to receive the names of those who wish to participate in the purchase of said property; and where maps can be seen, and all necessary information given.

The eligible situation of this property, and its convenience to the City by the facilities afforded by the railroad, render it one of the most desirable and valuable locations as a place of residence anywhere to be found in the vicinity of New York.

Persons wishing to examine the above property will find it a convenient hour to take the cars which leave City Hall either 10 o'clock A.M. or 1 ½ P.M. A person will be on the ground every day this week to make all necessary explanations. [n6 2t]   N. McGraw

• *New-York Daily Tribune*, December 21, 1868, pg. 8, col. 2:

Morrisania, N.Y. – The Eleventh Annual Ball of the Union Base Ball Club is announced for Christmas eve (sic), at Morrisania Hall…Mr. Brangman having resigned his position as member of the Board of Education, on account of removing to New-York City, Mr. T. Mason Oliver has been appointed to fill the vacancy.

This 1870 article in the *N.Y. Tribune* promotes the annexation to New York City of that portion of lower Westchester County that was to ultimately become the borough of the Bronx. This was written three years before actual annexation…

- *New-York Tribune*, New York, [N.Y.], Thursday, December 29, 1870 pg 4, col. 3:

LOWER WESTCHESTER – The enlargement of our City by the annexation of seven nearest townships of Westchester County, containing a population of 75,000, is recommended. That seems to us an excessive stride, yet *some* enlargement should be effected. Morrisania and the adjacent villages are virtually part of our city. Their connection with Westchester County is arbitrary and political merely. Their people mainly earn their living below Harlem Bridge: most of them come to the City weekly if not daily, and never go to White Plains unless at the sheriff's urgent solicitation.

The water-course known as Harlem River and in part Spuytenduyvel (sic) creek is no fit boundary for our City. It runs every way, but, for the greater part of its course, more nearly north and south than east and west, making our City nearly twice as long on its west as on its east side, and, for a considerable distance, a mere wooded ridge between the Hudson on the west and a paltry creek on the east. The Spuytenduyvel is, for most of its course, hardly navigable by a canoe, and is of no account in commerce...

What seems to us right and expedient is this: draw a line straight across Westchester County half a mile or so above Spuytenduyvel station on the Hudson River Railroad and set off all south of that line to our City leaving Yonkers (slightly curtailed) in Westchester with nearly all the villages which are now substantially independent. This line might be drawn a little higher or a little lower to conform it to existing township lines, or portions of West Farms and Westchester (townships) might be annexed to Eastchester and Yonkers, as should be found available.

The suggestion of a petty city of 40,000 people, composed of Morrisania, Westchester, and West Farms, seems to us most objectionable. It would involve a heavy expense for public edifices, surveys records &c., and, after this burdening the people heavily in the shape of taxes and debt; it would be absorbed by the Emporium. Whatever is ultimately best should be determined at once and forthwith carried into effect.

● *New-York Tribune*, August 2, 1860, pg. 7, col. 5:

The Morrisania Post-Office. – Complaints have reached us to the effect that the Post-Office at Morrisania is not properly managed. The surrounding population contains a large proportion of Germans. Yet, it is said that no information can be obtained as to the postal regulations between this and foreign countries, and letters, though frequently called for, are delayed in the office for weeks through negligence or indolence of those in charge.

● *New-York Tribune*, October 17, 1867, pg. 8, col. 3:

"Home News. The City," The new Harlem Bridge was thrown open to the public yesterday morning. At 10 o'clock Mayor Hoffman, accompanied by the Chairman of the Board of Supervisors of Westchester County, the President of the Board of Trustees of Morrisania, and the members of the Board of Commissioners of New-York with Alsop W. Lockwood, Commissioner of Westchester County, approached the bridge on the New-York side, and passed in triumph over to Westchester. After the transit, the party lunched with J.L. Mott, Esq. The Mayor was glad that the great connecting link between the Counties of New-York and Westchester had, after seven years, been completed. The company then toasted each other, and a gray-haired man who remembered the commencement of the enterprise, toasted the bridge.

• N.Y. Tribune, May 25, 1868, pg. 7, col. 1:

"General Real Estate Items" The Harlem Bridge, Morrisania, and Fordham Railroad Company have sold the lot 25 x 100 feet, at the intersection of Southern Boulevard and Boston Road, in Mott Haven, to Capt. Bowen, a wealthy real estate dealer of Mott Haven for $13,150. J.M. Beck has sold 300 feet front by 960 feet deep, Carr-ave (sic), Morrisania to the Ebbing Brothers of New-York, for $40,000.

• *New-York Tribune*, April 15, 1870, pg. 7, Col. 3:

TO LET – In West Morrisania within three minutes' walk of Melrose deport, a fine double HOUSE with good grounds and fruit trees: rent $850 per annum. Apply to Wm. C. Hyde No. 448 and 450 Broadway.

• *New-York Tribune*, December 6, 1867, pg. 8, col. 3:

MORRISANIA – The report of the Commissioners of Awards and Assessments on the Southern Boulevard shows the total amount to be $112,000, to be paid by property owners along the line…A cooperative store is proposed, and a meeting is to be held to-night for the purpose of organizing…Wendell Phillips will lecture on Friday evening in the Congressional

Meeting house before the Young Men's Literary Society, the subject being, "The Times."

- *New-York Tribune*, December 30, 1867, pg.2, col. 3:

Justice Dowling committed John Keefe, otherwise "Johnny, the Greek," to the Tombs, yesterday that malefactor having been arrested by Capt. John Jourdan on suspicion that he knew something of the street-car robbery of Mr. John S. Prouty of $6,000 worth of railway coupons and money...

- *The Sun*, New-York, [NY], Monday, August 2, 1869, pg.3, col. 3:

Justice in Morrisania -   The Westchester Office-Holders' Parade - The Absurd Growling of Tax-Payers - The Incorruptible Board of Trustees – The Battle of Police Justices – A Remarkable Protest from Justice Fuller – The Morrisania Police – Another Tempest in a Teapot.

Morrisania was made a corporation 3 or 4 years ago. This enabled the new town to indulge in the luxury of a Board of Trustees – a body of men that for learning, wit, probity, power, and honesty, can compare favorably with any similar institution in the world...the Board is composed of 8 freeholders who serve gratuitously...the Board lays out roads and streets, make repairs, construct school-houses; court-houses and bridges... the office of the Justice of the Peace is not a salaried position – depends on fees only.

- *The Sun*, New-York [NY], Monday, January 29, 1872, pg.1, col. 4:

"Westchester County" Yesterday Justice Hauptman of Morrisania held an inquest over the body of a man known only as "Dutch John," who died on North Brother Island, in Queens County, having been injured last night Thursday at Sobuckeke's Lager beer saloon in Morrisania. He was drunk and fell off a stoop, striking on the back part of his head. He was sent to the island. After his death he was held and the body was returned.

Every Sunday for months the neighborhood of Fifth street and Fordham avenue, Morrisania has been infested by a gang of young drunken firemen who insulted everybody. Yesterday a gang of these rowdies pitched on three or four inoffensive Germans as they were passing and beat them fearfully. Chief Dillert happened that way while the row was in progress and arrested George McFadden, George Stripling, and Walter Hunt, members of No. 1 engine. The rest escaped. Honest Justice Hauptman refused to take bail for them last night.

• Account of early baseball from *A Ball Player's Career: Being the Personal Experiences and Reminiscences of Adrian C. Anson* by Adrian C. Anson (late manager and captain of the Chicago Base Ball Club) 1900 [eBook Oct. 28, 2006 from Project Guttenberg - eBook #19652], Chapter III.—Some Facts about the National Game:

> The Athletics in 1866 played all of the strongest clubs in the country and were only twice defeated, once by the Atlantics of Brooklyn, andonce by the **Unions of Morrisania**. The first game between the Atlantics and Athletics for the championship took place October 1st, 1866, in Philadelphia, the number

of people present inside and outside the inclosed (sic) grounds being estimated as high as 30,000, it being the largest attendance known at the baseball game up to that time. Inside the inclosure (sic) the crowd was immense, and packed so close there was no room for the players to field. An attempt was made, however, to play the game, but one inning was sufficient to show that it was impossible, and after a vain attempt to clear the field both parties reluctantly consented to a postponement.

The postponed game was played October 22d, in Philadelphia.

The price of tickets was placed at one dollar and upwards, and two thousand people paid the "steep" price of admission, the highest ever charged for mere admission to the grounds, while five or six thousand more witnessed the game from the surrounding embankment. Rain and darkness obliged the umpire to call the game at the end of the second inning, the victory remaining with the Athletics, by the decisive totals of 31 to 12. A dispute about the gate money prevented the playing of the decisive game of the season.

The **Unions of Morrisania**, by defeating the Atlantics in two out of three games in the latter part of the season of 1867, became entitled to the nominal championship, which during the next two seasons was shifted back and forth between the leading clubs of New York and Brooklyn. The Athletics in 1868, and the Cincinnatis in 1869, had, however, the best records of their respective seasons, and were generally acknowledged as the virtual champions.

• *New York Tribune*, June 1, 1867: speaks of construction of a building: "Constructed of brick in the Norman style of architecture. The lower work is being done in imitation of free-stone, as well as the door frames, cornices, lintels, and all trimmings of the building...43 x 80 in size, with a tower 120 ' high...estimated cost $30,000.

• *New York Semi-Weekly Tribune*, April 2, 1867, pg. 2:

Base Ball

"In the game of Base Ball as now played we undoubtedly have a strictly National pastime (sic). What cricket is to an Englishman, base ball is to an American. Unreflecting people may regard base ball as "a very good thing for boys, perhaps," or, a suitable sport to "pass away an idle hour or so on a holiday." Those, however, who intelligently consider the matter, see in this game the means to an end which has been sought for in vain for years past on this side of the Atlantic, the end in view being the popularizing of physical education and healthy out-door exercise and sport...

"...Since the close of the year of he war of the Rebellion the game has made great strides in popularity, North, East, South and West. Especially in the South and West has base ball become popular, and probably nothing could have been introduced into the South better calculated to benefit Southern young men than this our now National game (sic)...

"…The season of 1867 will soon be commenced and the prospects are that it will be fully as interesting as any we have had. In New-York, our city clubs are gathering their clans for the Summer campaign, and as soon as good weather sets in, and old Winter has ceased further dalliance with fair Spring, we shall see the various ball grounds placed in proper condition, and crowds of ball-players on them busily engaged in ball-play…

"…The Union Club of Morrisania, the rival of the Mutuals for metropolitan supremacy, will occupy its old grounds this year, the club being unable to procure a locality suitable for a permanent ball-ground as was anticipated. The Union nine will include Birdsall, Pabor, Smith, Martin, Goldie, Hannegan, Akin, Austin and Hudson. [George] Wright, we believe, has joined an out-of-town club…

"…The Hoboken grounds are reached by the Barclay-st. ferry, and by cars to the Elysian Fields. The Second-ave. cars go direct to the Red House Grounds, and the Harlem Railroad passes Morrisania…"

APPENDIX II

NOTES:

The Baseball Field in the 1840s and '50s

In general, the field was smaller. The distance between bases was 42 paces, which at that time was approximately 74'. The distance between home plate and second base was approximately 105' with a pitching line 12' wide located halfway between. The equivalent of today's foul poles were located 100' from home plate. Cartwright established the diamond shape field we are familiar with today.

In 1857, the distance between bases was officially set at 90' and the pitching line at 45'. The distance of ninety feet turned out to be perfect, because the results would always be in doubt. Any shorter and runner would most likely always be safe on close plays, any further, he would have no chance of reaching the base in time.

The Equipment

Until 1867 when bats were limited to a 42 inch length, they could be of any size, weight, and diameter, with bats up to 50" or more in length not uncommon.

The balls used were smaller, lighter, and softer than modern ones. They were handmade, consisting of yarn or string wrapped around any type of solid core and covered with brown leather. The same ball usually was in play the entire game.

A National Association of Base Ball Players rule (New York, March 14th 1860) specifies that "The ball must weigh not less than five and three-fourths, nor more than six ounces avoirdupois. It must measure not less than nine and three-fourths, nor more than ten inches in circumference. It must be composed of India rubber and yarn, and covered with leather, and, in all match games, shall be furnished by the challenging club, and become the property of the winning club, as a trophy of victory." These specs would change in years to come.

Gloves were not used in the 1840s and 1850s, and did not come into general use until the 1870s. Even then, they resembled golf gloves, being used to relieve the sting of the ball rather than as a aid in catching. Padded gloves did not appear until the 1880s, and as late as the 1890s some players still played without any gloves.

Baseballs

Early baseballs were homemade. These early balls were called "belt," or "belted balls" so named due to the design of the stitching which resembles an "H" in the center. Normally comprised of just one strip of leather, the "belt" ball is a variation of that design and was crafted using four separate pieces of leather. In the late 1850s the National Association of Baseball Players changed the standard specifications of a regulation ball. The new rules required that the baseball weigh 6.25 ounces (up from the previous standard of 5.5 ounces) and have a circumference of 10.25 inches (as opposed to the earlier measurement of 9 inches). Some, like the one in the photo measured eight inches in circumference and weighed just 2.4 ounces, which indicates that it probably dates prior to that rule change, perhaps even much earlier.

By 1871, there were six manufacturers of baseballs in New York City supplying the surrounding teams. Prices varied from $18 to $5 a dozen. These were wound rubber wrapped in wool yarn by male workers. The cover was horse-hide put on by women using a saddler's needle and saddler's thread. (According to the *N.Y. Times*, April 30, 1871).

A homemade baseball, commonly referred to as a "belt" or "belted" ball, c. early 1850s

Batters (or Strikers), Pitchers

The striker was allowed up to three swings at the ball no matter how many pitches were delivered. The batter had the privilege to ask the pitcher to throw at a requested location over the plate. There were no called strikes or balls. The batter could stand there all day waiting for the pitch he wanted while he wore out the pitcher. This is why baseball sores were so high, 50 or 60 runs being scored by one side alone was not unusual. The idea of called strikes was not introduced until 1858. Five years later, umpires were allowed to call "unfair pitches" (balls). For several years, it only took three balls to constitute a walk. With the introduction of these new rules, the scores were more in line with today's game stats.

There were three ways that a striker could commit an out: (1) By grounding out; (2) having a hit ball caught on the fly or on the first bounce; or (3) being thrown out by the catcher after missing his third swing (he was allowed to try to reach first base whether the catcher caught the ball or not). One of the original Cartwright rules that is still in use to this day: if the catcher drops the ball on a called third strike or a swing and a miss, the batter can run to first and has to be thrown or tagged out before he reaches first base.

Pitchers could only throw underhand in a straight arm motion perpendicularly to the ground. Sidearm deliveries were first allowed in 1874 and overhand pitches, at least in the National League, a decade later. There was no pitching mound, that not coming along until the 20th Century.

Pitchers could take a running start toward the pitching line before delivering the ball. A balk could be called if he crossed the line before the ball was released. This running was curtailed years later when various size "pitching boxes" were tried. The first pitching rubber did not appear until 1893.

Hitting a batter or being hit by a pitched ball was used by both the pitcher and batter as an important part of the games strategy. The pitchers continually attempted to intimidate batters by throwing at them. Pitchers would also attempt to hit batters to prevent base runners from stealing bases and the batters would obviously attempt to avoid the pitched ball with runners on base.

Stealing a base was somewhat of a novelty in the '50s and '60s. For a time, stolen bases were credited when a base runner reached an extra base on a base hit from another player. For example if a runner on first base reached on a single, it would count as a steal.

Beginning with the 1870 season the first pitched ball to the batter was not counted. Neither the batter nor the pitcher received a warning before a strike or ball was called. In 1874, every third "unfair" pitch was called a ball, technically allowing the pitcher to throw nine unfair pitches to give the batter his base on balls.

Speechless communication and silent instructions (Baseball Sign Language):

In Paul Dickson's *"The Hidden Language of Baseball,"* (Walker & Co., 2005) he traces the origin of how sign language became an integral part of the game. According to Dickson, baseball's tradition of signing grew out of the signal flags used by ships and soldiers' hand signals during battle. They were first used in games during the Civil War, and then professionally by the Cincinnati Red Stockings, in 1869.* Seven years later, the Hartford Dark Blues appear to be the first team to steal signs. He thoroughly researched accounts of the game's idiosyncratic forms of communication. Baseball is set apart from other sports by the use of a distinctive coded language on the field.

> * There is, however, an account of a game played between the Excelsiors and the Flour City Base Ball Club, in the Rochester *Evening Express*, July 9, 1860 in which there was a reference to signals being employed.

Dickson reveals a short but thorough history of baseball as seen through the development of signs, sign stealing and 'tip-off' reading. It has become a rich unspoken sign language that has guided the course of the game for almost 150 years. It is one of the elements that distinguishes baseball from other games. Harry Wright and his brother George Wright of the Cincinnati Red Stockings were masters of defensive shifts using signals to conduct activity on the field, like having an infielder drop a pop-up to enable a double-play (before the 'infield fly rule' was put into effect), or having the catcher intentionally drop a third strike with a runner on first to initiate a double play. Harry Wright also had his "strikers" hit to specific locations. Darryl Block, the novelist in his book *If I Never Get Back,* discovered a citation dealing with this Cincinnati style of baseball. He states, "I imagine hat signs, vocal or otherwise, might have been used in all of these maneuvers..."

DUMMY HOY   CF

"Dummy" Hoy – 1887

Umpires had their own set of hand signals to announce their decisions for safe, outs, strikes, balls, fouls et. al.. There is still much debate as to how this got started. The most generally accepted theory concerns one William Ellsworth "Dummy" Hoy (1861 – 1961), a deaf ballplayer whose career spanned the years from 1888 to 1902. He played mostly for the Cincinnati Reds and Washington, D.C. franchises. Pitchers took advantage of him because while batting, he had to ask the umpire if it was a called strike or ball. This distracted him and his batting average suffered. One day he came up with an idea to have his third base coach signal the balls and strikes (raising the right hand for a strike, and the left for a ball) and thus he was able to concentrate on the next pitch. The umpires picked it up and began to use the signals themselves. The spectators and sportswriters loved the idea also. It made it easier to follow the game pitch for pitch. Other signs were developed to call a runner safe or out, a ball fair or foul etc. And so these signals were universally adopted by the umpires and the league.

Union of Morrisania won – lost record prior to the NABBP:

10/25/1855 defeated the Young America (New York) 25 – 8
07/31/1856 defeated the Baltics (NY) 23 – 17
08/27/1856 defeated the Baltics (NY) 15 – 12
09/17/1856 lost to the Eckfords (Bklyn) 22 – 8
09/25/1856 defeated the Baltics (NY) 25 – 11
10/15/1856 lost to the Eckfords (Bklyn) 22 – 6

Source: Wright, Marshall D., *The National Association of Base Ball Players, 1857 – 1870,* (2000) McFarland & Company, Inc.

APPENDIX III

LINE UPS AND ROSTERS OF THE UNION CLUB

Union of Morrisania won – lost record prior to the NABBP:

10/25/1855 defeated the Young America (New York) 25 – 8
07/31/1856 defeated the Baltics (NY) 23 – 17
08/27/1856 defeated the Baltics (NY) 15 – 12
09/17/1856 lost to the Eckfords (Bklyn) 22 – 8
09/25/1856 defeated the Baltics (NY) 25 – 11
10/15/1856 lost to the Eckfords (Bklyn) 22 – 6

Source: Wright, Marshall D., *The National Association of Base Ball Players, 1857 – 1870,* (2000) McFarland & Company, Inc.

Lineups and Rosters, as a member of the NABBP

1857

Booth, 1b
Balcolm, 2b
Ferdon, ss
Todd 3b, c
E. Durell of, 2b
Rodman, of
Dickerson, of
Gifford, c

Pinckney, p
Roosa, 3b
Henry, of
Mann, -
Brandon, 1b
Tremper, of

Frisbe, -

1858

Fredon, 1b, ss
Pinckney, 2b
Brandow, ss
Todd, 3b
Dickinson, of
Parker, of
Balcolm, of
Booth, c
Gifford, p
 E. Durrell, 1b

1859

Parker, 1b
William Abrams, 2b
Bogle, ss
Bennett, 3b
Bernard Hannegan, of
Booth, of

Balcom, of
Gifford, c
Pinckney, p

1860

Gifford, 1b
Wm. Abrams, 2b, c, 3b
Bogle, ss
Bennett, 3b
Balcom, of
Bernard Hannegan, of, p
E. Durell, of, 2b
Pinckney, p, 2b

Todd, of
Kinloch, of, 3b
Borland, 3b
Albro
Jackson
Frisbee
Milliken
Mallory
Stearns
Valentine

1861

No information available (Beginning of the Civil War depleted many rosters)

1862

E. Durell, 1b
Pinckney, 2b
Bassford, ss, of
Hyatt, 3b, ss, of
Nicholson, of, 2b
Sammy Collins, of
Albro, of, 3b
Wm. Abrams, c, ss
Bernard Hannegan, p

Bogle, 2b
Gaynor, c
Van Horn, of
F. Durrell, of
Parker, ss

1863

Wm. Abrams
B. Hannegan
Nicholson
Dave Birdsall
Hyatt
Sammy Collins

1864

The 'fly game,' came into vogue.

Dave Birdsall
Bernard Hannegan
E. Durell
W.F. Hudson
Sammy Collins
Wm. Abrams
Bogle

1865

George Smith, 1b
Harley Pabor, 2b, of
Bernard Hannegan ss, 2b, of, 3b
Nicholson 3b, 2b
E. Durell, of, 2b
W.F. Hudson, of, 2b, ss
Dan Ketchum, of, ss
Dave Birdsall, c, p
Sammy Collins, p
William Abrams, of, 3b
Henry Austin, 2b, of

1865 Union lineup from *The N. Y. Tribune*, August 21, 1865
Hudson, rf
Smith, 1b

Durell, lf
Hannegan, ss
Nicholson, 3b
Birdsall, c
Ketchum, cf
Pabor, 2b
"Sam", p

1866

George Smith, 1b, of
Al Martin, 2b, of
Bernard Hannegan, ss, of
William Abrams, 3b
Dan ketchum, of, 2b, 3b
Henry Austin, of
Albro Aiken, of, c, ss
Dave Bridsall, c
Charley Pabor, p

W. F. Hudson, of, 3b
George Wright, ss, c
John Goldie, 1b

1867

John Goldie, 1b
Al Martin, 2b
George Smith, ss, of, c, 1b
Dan Ketchum, 3b

Albro Aiken, of, ss
Tommy Beals, of
Dave Birdsall, c
Charley Pabor, p

Hudson, of
William Abrams, of
Norton, p

1868

John Goldie, 1b
Al Martin, 2b
George Wright, ss, 2b

Ed Shelley, 3b, 2b
Henry Austin, of
George Smith, of, 1b
Reynolds, of
Dave Birdsall, c
Charley Pabor, p
Steve Bellan, 2b, of

1869

Baker, 1b, of
John Goldie, 2b, 1b
Tom Haines, ss
Weidberg, 3b, of
Harry Austin, of, 2b, c

Whelan, of, 3b, 1b
Ten Eyke, of, 3b
Carsie, c
Lyons, p, of

Reynolds, 2b, ss
George Smith, 3b, of, 1b

1870

Brown, 1b
Dick Higam, 2b
John Bass, ss
Ed Shelley, 3b
Al Gedney, of
Henry Austin, of
John Kenney, of, 3b
Dave Birdsall, c
Charley Pabor, p

Reynolds, of
Jim Holdsworth, 3b
Charley Bearman, 1b

APPENDIX IV

EXCERPTS FROM CRAIG WAFF'S GAME TABULATIONS
Games Tab: Greater New York City (from1845 to 1860)
Complete file can be found on Protoball.org

1855

Oct. 22 or 25, 1855: Union (Morrisania) 25 – Young America [Harlem, N.Y.] at Morrisania (6 innings)

> Sources: 1) "Base Ball: Young America vs. Union," *The Spirit of the Times,* Vol. 25, no. 38, November 1855, p. 45, col. 1; 2) Peverelly, p. 49; Orem, p. 14; 4) Wright, p.5

1856

July 31, 1856 (Thur.): at Harlem grounds, Red House. Union (Morrisania) 23 – Baltic (NY) 17, (6 innings). (*New York Clipper*: "The match…was one of the most interesting and exciting games at base ball that has been played for some time. The occasion attracted a large assemblage of spectators, including representatives from all the clubs of New York and Brooklyn, and as it was generally understood that the contesting clubs were about evenly matched as regards age and experience in the game, additional interest was felt by all present in the result…")

Sources: 1) "New –York City: Base Ball," *New York Daily Times,* vol. 5, no. 1520 (2 Aug. 1856), p. 6, col. 1; 2) *New York Sunday Mercury*, 3 Aug. 1856 [NOT YET SEEN]; 3) "Unions and Baltics," *New York Clipper*, vol.4, no. 16 (9 Aug. 1856), p. 123, col. [xx]; 4) *New York Sunday Mercury*, list; 5) W. M. Rankin, *"Early History of Baseball,"* (1886), clipping in the Mears Collection; 6) Peverelly, p. 49; 7) Wright, pp. 5 & 6.

August 27, 1856 (Wed.): at Morrisania. Union (Morrisania) 15, Baltic (NY) 12 (5 innings – return match – drawn game due to darkness).

Sources: 1) "Union vs. Baltic," *New York Clipper,* vol. 4, no. 20 (6 Sept. 1856), p. 155, col. [xx]; 2) *New York Sunday Mercury*, list; 3) Peverelly p. 49; 4) Wright, pp. 5 & 6.

September 20, 1856 (Sat.): at Harlem Red House or Morrisania (*N.Y. Sunday Mercury*) Enterprise Jrs. Of Morrisania, 25 – Young America (Harlem) 9; 5 innings (*Porters Spirit of the Times:* "Both of the clubs are composed of lads between the age of fifteen and eighteen years; and there is some very good players among them.")

Sources: 1) "Base Ball," *Porter's Spirit of the Times,* Vol. 1, no. 3 (20 Sept. 1856), p. 37, col.3; 2) "Enterprise vs. Young America," *N.Y. Clipper* Vol. 4, no. 23 (27 Sept. 1856), p.183, col. [xx]; 3) "Base Ball," *Porter's Spirit of the Times,* Vol. 1, no. 4, (27

Sept. 1856), p.53, col. 2

October 4, 1856 (Sat.): at Morrisania. Enterprise Jr. (Morrisania) 7 – Young America Jr. (Harlem) 6 (5 innings – return match – drawn game, stopped due to darkness). (*Porter's Spirit of the Times:* The teams "did not conclude their game, as it became dark when the fifth innings had been called out. At that part of the game the young 'uns were in a minority of one.")

> Sources: 1) Enterprise of Morrisania vs. Young America of Harlem," *New York Clipper* Vol. 4, no. 25 (11 Oct. 1856), p. 195, col. [xx]; 2) "Base Ball," *Porter's Spirit of the Times,* Vol. 1, no. 6 (11 Oct. 1856), p. 93, col.3; 3) *New York Sunday Mercury,* list (Enterprise – 8 runs)

October 11, 1856 (Sat.): at Morrisania. Enterprise Jr. (Morrisania) 20 – Young America Jr. (Harlem) 19, (10 innings – drawn game)

> Sources: 1) "Base Ball," *Porter's Spirit of the Times,* Vol. 1, no. 7 (18 Oct. 1856) p. 117, col.1; 2) *New York Sunday Mercury*, list

October 15, 1856 (Wed.): at Harlem Red House. Eckford (Brooklyn) 22 – Union (Morrisania) 6 (4 innings – return match). (*Porter's Spirit of the Times* "A bad closing mate: this for a young club like the Union; but if they practice with perseverance before the next season, they can and will do better.")

Sources: 1) "Union vs. Eckford," *New York Clipper*, Vol. 4, no. 27 (25 Oct. 1856) p. 211, col. [xx]; 2) "Base Ball," *Porter's Spirit of the Times*, Vol. 1, no. 8 (25 Oct. 1856), p. 133, col. 2; 3) *New York Sunday Mercury* list (Union – 7runs); 4) Peverelly, pp. 49 & 73; 5) Wright, pp. 5 & 6.

1857

September 16, 1857 (Wed.): at Union (Morrisania). Union (Morrisania) 30 – Excelsior (South Brooklyn) 8 (*Porter's Spirit of the Times*: "The 15th will be a grand gala day in Morrisania, the occasion being the anniversary celebration of the founding of that village.")

Sources: 1) "Out-Door Sports: Base Ball: Matches to Come." *Porter's Spirit of the Times*, vol. 3, no. 1 (5 Sept. 1857), p. 4, col.1; 2) "Excelsior vs. Union," New York Clipper, vol. 5, no.23 (26 Sept. 1857), p. 183, col. [xx] [The baseball Index; NOT YET SEEN]; 3) Peverelly, pp. 49 & 53; 4) Wright, pp. 11 & 13.

1858

August 5, 1858 (Thur): at Morrisania Union grounds on the margin of the railroad, near the Melrose station. Union (Morrisania) 33, Adriatic (Newark) 16.

Sources: 1) "Base Ball," *Brooklyn Daily Eagle*, vol. 17, no. 181 (2 Aug. 1858), p. 2, col. 5; 2) "Out-Door Sports: Base Ball: Union vs. Adriatic," Porter's Spirit of the Times, vol.4, no 24 (14 Aug. 1858), p. 380, col. 2.

Oct. 23, 1858 (Sat.): at Active grounds, 114th St. Active (Harlem) 48, Enterprise [Sr.] (Morrisania) 11

> Sources: 1) "Out-Door Sports: Base Ball: Matches to Come," Porter's Spirit of the Times, vol. 5, no.8 (23 Oct. 1858), p. 116, col.2; 2) Dutchman, "Out-Door Sports: Base-Ball: Actives vs. Enterprise," *Porter's Spirit of the Times*, vol. 5, no.9 (30 Oct. 1858), p. 135, col. 1.

1859

Oct. 5, 1859 (Wed.): at Morrisania Union grounds. Union (Morrisania) 19 – Excelsior (South Brooklyn) 15. [An inscribed gold-painted, "lemon-peel" ball was awarded to the victors, the Union Club, as a trophy].

> Sources: Peverelly, pp. 49 & 53; 2) Wright, pp.31 & 36.

Prior to Oct. 8, 1859: at Champion (NY)? Enterprise (Morrisania)

> Source: Champion, of New York vs. Enterprise of Morrisania," *Wilkes' Spirit of the Times,* vol.1, no. 5 (8 Oct. 1859), p. 70, col. [xx] [The baseball Index – NOT YET SEEN]

1860

June 8, 1860 (Fri.): Bedford, L.I. Atlantic grounds. Atlantic (Brooklyn) 15 – Union (Morrisania) 4. (*Brooklyn Daily Eagle*: "Only five innings on each side were played, as the tornado of dust that came up about 4 o'clock interrupted the proceedings, and the rain that followed shortly afterward, put a stop to the play. About 4,000 people were collected on the grounds, and quite a bevy of the fair ladies of this city occupied the seats the Atlantics had naturally provided for them. Admirable order was kept on the ground by the members of the Club, and but for the weather everything would have passed off pleasantly.") (*New York Clipper*: called on account of "sudden storm of wind, dust, and rain"…"Nearly 5,000 people were present.")

> Sources: 1) "City News and Gossip: Atlantic of Brooklyn vs. Union of Morrisania," *Brooklyn Daily Eagle*, vol.19, no 137 (9 June 1860), p. 3, col. 1; 2) "Atlantic vs. Union," *New York Clipper*, vol. 8, no.10 (23 June, 1860), p. 76, col. [xx]; 3) Peverelly, pp. 49 & 63; 4) Wright, pp. 45 & 49.

Prior to June 16, 1860: at Rose Hill or Social?

> Source: "Rose Hill vs. Social," New York Clipper, vol. 8, no. 9 (16 June 1860), p. 69, col. [xx] [The Baseball Index - NOT YET SEEN]

August 8, 1860 (Wed.): at Railroad Ave. Union (Morrisania (W), Adriatic (L).

> Source: "Base Ball," Newark Daily Advertiser, vol. 29, no. 188 (9 Aug. 1860), p. 2, col. 5.

Aug. 30, 1860 (Thur.): Buena (Mott Haven) vs. Newark Jr. (Newark) (scheduled)

> Sources: 1) "Base Ball," *Newark Daily Advertiser,* vol. 29, no. 206 (29 Aug, 1860), p. 2, col. 5; 2) "Base Ball," *Newark Daily Advertiser*, vol. 29, no. 223 (18 Sept. 1860), p. 2, col. 5 [no date provided].

September 7, 1860 (Fri.): at Morrisania Union grounds. Excelsior (Brooklyn) 7 – Union (Morrisania) 4 (return or home-and home match) (*New York Times*: "One of the best contested games of Base Ball that has ever taken place in this vicinity...one of the smallest scores on record. The fielding on both sides were of the very highest order, the out-fielding being without a flaw, the catching excellent, and the pitching on both sides unusually fine, the muffs being almost entirely confined to the bases...There were not less than 500 spectators on the ground, of whom an unusually large proportion were ladies.")

(*New York Clipper:*" One of the best contested matches of the season...a close game of...two hours and twenty-five minutes duration. The Excelsiors, for the first time this season, were recipients of similar treatment to that they have been in the habit of giving to others, their score of "runs in each innings" being marked with no less than five ciphers, and their total score of runs being the small figure of 7! – the lowest score they have ever made in a match...The Excelsiors were most hospitably entertained, and the day's play terminated with a lively interchange of speeches, songs, and sentiment, characteristic of the forensic and vocal talent possessed by the respective clubs.")

Sources: 1) "Base Ball: Union, of Morrisania vs. Excelsior, of South Brooklyn – Excelsior 7; Union 4," *New York Times*, vol.9, no 2798 (8 Sep. 1860), p. 8, col.5; 2) "Excelsior vs. Union," *New York Clipper*, Vol. 8, no.23 (22 Sep 1860), p. 180, col.[xx]; 3) Peverelly, pp. 49 & 53 [former states 4 runs for Excelsior]; 4) Wright, pp. 44 & 49.

September 15, 1860 (Sat.): at Morrisania Union grounds. Putnam (Brooklyn) 12 – Union (Morrisania) 6 (return match) (*New York Times*; "a protracted game of more than three hours' duration...It has been the good fortune of the Union Club to be a participant in some of the best games on record, and though of late quite unsuccessful, yet they have always require a strong team to overcome them.")

(*New York Clipper*: "The interest of the game was destroyed by the delays that occurred in consequence of several of the strikers on the Putnam side, and on two on the part of the Unions, waiting an unusual time at the bat for a particular kind of ball. The Putnams commenced it, and the Unions followed suit, and this led to unpleasant feelings. There is nothing that is calculated to impart interest to a game so much as promptitude in striking at the first ball within reach, and the most ungenerous and unmanly style of play is that plan of waiting at the bat until players on the bases make their runs; it is contemptible in the extreme. A good batsman is never guilty of it; it is only poor batsmen that wait for particular balls...")

Sources: 1) "Base Ball," *Brooklyn Daily Eagle*, vol. 19, no. 222 (17 Sep 1860), p.3, col. 3; 2) "Field Sports: Base Ball: Putnam, of Brooklyn, vs. Union of

Morrisania," *New York Times*, vol. 9, no. 2805 (17 Sep 1860) p. 8, col. 5; 3) "Union vs. Putnam," *New York Clipper*. [?] Sep 1860; 4) Peverelly, p. 49; 5) Wright, pp. 48 & 49

September 19, 1860 (Wed.): at Greenpoint Eckford grounds. Eckford (Brooklyn) 41 – Union (Morrisania) 5 (*New York Times*: "A somewhat amusing game of ball was played... Owing to the prospect of rain but four of the Union first nine were on the ground, and they were compelled to call on five of their 'muffins' for assistance. As might be expected the muffins play predominantly among the Unions, some of the points played by the substitutes elicited general laughter and applause.")

Sources: 1) "Base Ball: Eckford, of Brooklyn, vs. Union of Morrisania," *New York Times,* vol. 9, no. 2808 (20 Sep 1860), p 8, col. 4; 2) Peverelly, pp. 49 & 74; 3) Wright, pp. 44 & 49.

SELECTED BIBLIOGRAPHY
AND RECOMMENDED READING

Adams, D. L., et al. (1854) The New York Baseball Rules. *The Book of American Pastimes.* New York

Adelman, M. A. (1980) "The First Baseball Game, the Newspaper References to Baseball, and the New York Club" *Journal of Sport History.* (Winter)

The Baseball Encyclopedia : The Complete and Definitive Record of Major League Baseball, Macmillan, 1968, 1976, 1982, 1993, 1996

Block, David, *Baseball Before We Knew It: A Search for the Roots of the Game,* Lincoln, University of Nebraska Press, 2005

Goldstein, Warren, *Playing for Keeps: A History of Early Baseball, 20th Anniversary Edition,* Cornell University Press, March 12, 2009

Henderson, Robert W., *Ball, Bat and Bishop: The Origin of Ball Games*, New York, Rockport Press, 1947 [the genealogy was established definitively by Henderson].

Morris, Peter, *But Didn't We Have Fun? An Informal History of Baseball's Pioneer Era 1843 – 1870,* Ivan R. Dee (March 16, 2010, 296 pp. Morris explores the earliest days of baseball through the voices of players and journalists who wrote about it in the 27-year period in the mid-19th century before professional baseball emerged.

_____., *A Game of Inches: The Stories Behind the Innovations that Shaped Baseball: The game in the Field (Vol. I)*, 533 pp., Ivan R. Dee Publisher (March 23, 2006). The scope of *A Game of Inches* is encyclopedic, with nearly a thousand entries that illuminate the origins of items ranging from catchers' masks to hook slides to intentional walks to cork-center baseballs. But this is much more than just a reference guide.

_____., editor & others, *Base Ball Founders: The Clubs, Players and Cities of the Northeast That Established the Game.* McFarland, May 2013, illus., notes, bibliog., index. This is the second of two ambitious volumes on the earliest history of baseball compiled by scholars affiliated with the Society for American Baseball Research, including Gregory Christiano who has contributed articles on the Eagle, Active and Empire Base Ball Clubs of the 1850s and '60s. Along with team histories, this volume includes brief biographies of scores of players and club officials, and provides a comprehensive reference source on the genesis of baseball

Nemec, David, *The Rank and File of 19th Century Major League Baseball: Biographies of 1,084 Players, Owners, Managers and Umpires* [Paperback] McFarland (March 20, 2012) Foreword by John Thorn.

Orem, Preston D, *Baseball, from the Newspaper Accounts* (Altadena, Calif.: self-published, 1961)

Peverelly, Charles A., *The Book of American Pastimes*, New York, self-published, 1866

Peverelly's compilation has been reprinted as *Peverelly's National Game*, ed. by John Freyer and Mark Rucker (Charleston, S.C.: Arcadia Publishing, 2005).

Ryczek, William J., *Baseball's First Inning: A History of the National Pastime Through the Civil War,* McFarland, March 13, 2009

Sullivan, Dean A., compiler and editor, *Early Innings: A Documentary History of Baseball 1825 – 1908* (Lincoln: Univ. of Nebraska Press (1995).

Thorn, John, *Baseball in the Garden of Eden: The Secret History of the Early Game* Simon & Schuster (March 15, 2011). John Thorn, baseball's preeminent historian, examines the creation story of the game.

_____. *Baseball: Our Game*, Thinker Media, Inc. (November 15, 2011) John Thorn, Official Historian for Major League Baseball, tracks the history of the game in America from its misty origins to present-day glory. This edition explores the evolution of America's National Pastime through cultural shifts and significant changes in the game.

Wright, Marshall D., *The National Association of Base Ball Players, 1857 – 1870* McFarland & Company, Inc. Publishers 2000

What better way to sum up the game of baseball than a passage from A. Bartlett Giamatti, "The Green Fields of the Mind:"

"It breaks your heart.
It is designed to break your heart.
The game begins in the spring
when everything else begins again,
and, it blossoms in the summer,
filling the afternoons and evenings,
and then as soon as the
chill rains come, it stops
and leaves you to face
the fall alone. You count
on it, rely on it to buffer
the passage of time,
to keep the memory of
sunshine and high skies
alive, and then just when
the days are all twilight,
when you need it most,
it stops."

- A. Bartlett Giamatti

(Yale Alumni Magazine, November 1977)
From "A Great and Glorious Game: Baseball Writings
of A. Bartlett Giamatti"
"The Green Fields of the Mind"

Angelo Bartlett "Bart" Giamatti (April 4, 1938 – September 1, 1989) was the president of Yale University, president of the National League,1986 and later the seventh Commissioner of Major League Baseball in 1989. He died of a heart attack six months into his presidency at only fifty-one years old.

Books by Gregory J. Christiano

Sworn to Remember, A Personal History and Memoir of Gregory J. Christiano Second Printing, (2013) 556 pages (Illustrated) – The autobiography of Mr. Christiano (1947 -) – his reminiscences of what it was like growing up in the Bronx, his college years in Iowa, his career path when he returned to New York City and other chapters covering his family and friends. Much of the book explains how he and his wife still struggle to raise two handicapped daughters. This is not just another family history, but an account of one person's perspective on life and its challenges.

Fast Page Notes on Sworn to Remember (2011) 212 pp. A synopsis of Gregory's autobiography chapter for chapter. It's a quick guide summarizing the details of each stage in his life. Included are character sketches of his family and friends. The reader will get an overall picture of one man's journey through life.

Trial by Terror, and Other Short Stories (2011) 268 pages – A collection of fifty short stories covering many genres: passionate crime and romance, science fiction thrills and personal dramas, westerns to the shrill cry of horror. Written in easy to read prose, the stories are unconventional and entertaining.

Conversations from the Past (2007) (Illustrated) 276 pp. Love, humor, heartbreak resonate from the past with lilting rhymes and lucid prose. This collection of poetry, short stories and essays will grip the reader with topics that are lighthearted and wistful as well as terrifying and intriguing.

A Night on Mystical Mountain, Selected Poems and Short Stories (2005) (Illustrated) 225 pp. Epic poetry and powerful short stories carry the reader into mysterious journeys through dark city streets, into a medieval manor house, up an enchanted valley and down the path of a secluded garden. There is fantasy and magic to thrill and hold the reader spellbound.

Baseball in the Bronx, Before the Yankees (2013) (Illustrated) Baseball in the mid-nineteenth century evolved into the beloved game we know today. The region north of the Harlem River, eventually becoming the borough of the Bronx, played an important role in that development. This narrative non-fiction takes us through those early years explaining the struggles and triumphs, the trial and error with a host of colorful characters along the way.

Would you like to see your manuscript become a book?

If you are interested in becoming a PublishAmerica author, please submit your manuscript for possible publication to us at:

acquisitions@publishamerica.com

You may also mail in your manuscript to:

**PublishAmerica
PO Box 151
Frederick, MD 21705**

We also offer free graphics for Children's Picture Books!

---

www.publishamerica.com

CPSIA information can be obtained at www.ICGtesting.com
Printed in the USA
BVOW031208300613

324652BV00001B/52/P